# How to Beat the Biscuit Tin Blues

### Gina Battye

# Copyright

## Dedication

This book is dedicated to you.

For taking that step to become healthier and happier.

To Karl,

Wishing you great health,
wealth + happiness!

All the very best with your

story :)

Gina /x

## What People Are Saying

"Loved it, loved it, loved it! Finally, a self-help book that actually works. Nicely-written and cheerily, refreshingly free of celebrity ego or pseudo-science, based on common sense and achievable goals."

**Joanne Harris, international best-selling author**

"This is the ONLY book you'll ever need to banish sugar cravings forever. There are no complicated meal plans or time-consuming exercise regimes here. This book is packed full of practical tips to help you gain control over your eating, so that you have all the energy and vitality you'll ever need. Gina has produced a 'must-have' guide for anyone who finds themselves reaching for cookies or chocolate throughout the day. Inspirational!"

**Stephanie J. Hale, author of *'Millionaire Women, Millionaire You'*, www.stephaniejhale.com**

"WELL - that makes it really simple doesn't it? We usually plan everything we're going to do during the day …EXCEPT the thing that makes us FIT enough to out manoeuvre the schedules in the FIRST PLACE…FEED OURSELVES PROPERLY. BUY THIS…READ IT - and do what Gina tells you!!!"

**Nicky Pattinson, sales speaker, writer and sales turnaround consultant**

"I have read many nutrition books over the years. I am qualified in this field myself and I have to say that *"How to Beat the Biscuit Tin Blues"* is a truly enjoyable and informative read. It is straight to the point and does not go around the houses. It delivers facts in an easy, quick and understandable way. Most books I have read that cover this area go into far too much depth. I like that Gina has put things into simple terms that will ensure this book is not daunting to anyone reading it. I will be recommending this to my clients!"

**Sonia Armitage, figure bodybuilding competitor and Pro-Standard Sponsored Athlete.**

"What a refreshing change to read a book that gives you tools and techniques to actually achieve a more healthy life. Positive Image is such an important message and this book can really help inspire people to put basic actions in place to make a difference. Well done Gina!"

**Kate Hardcastle, award winning business woman, entrepreneur, campaigner and mum**

"Superb! If you want to change your lifestyle, then this is the book for you, An easy to read book that is both enjoyable and thought provoking, with practical tips to follow in your daily life."

**Collette Whiteley, inspirational leader within global banking.**

"During my working life I have faced many of the challenges referred to in Gina's book. This book provides a straight forward guide on how to survive in a healthy and more enjoyable manner in today's 24 x7 world. There are no complex 'science' terms used, just lots of great simple and effective 'tips' that are summarised at the end of each chapter. This makes it easier to refer to in the future."

**Richard Evers, Hewlett-Packard – manager and business mentor**

"This is a very enjoyable and informative book, full of wisdom and down-to-earth advice on how to get fitter, healthier and live a calmer life. It's already brought changes to my life and will continue to do so."

**Tim Russell, editor, writer and proofreader of award-winning magazines and newspapers.**

# Table of Contents

# Thank you

This is it! I started this project thinking I would like to write something that would help my family and friends to make some simple changes to their life. The idea was to share what I have learnt and applied to my life in hope it would help them to become healthier and happier too. This is the result and what a journey it has been!

I am humbled by all the support and well wishes I have had during the writing process. I would like to express my thanks here to those that have helped to shape my life as well as this book.

**Firstly, to my mum and dad** for bringing me into this world. You are amazing and I love you so much. You have been there with me through everything. I cannot express in words how much that means to me. Thank you for your continued support, your wisdom and your love. I am looking forward to sharing the next chapter of my life with you.

**To my grandparents.** Thank you for looking after me when I was young, nurturing me when I was a bit older and for all the lessons you have shared with me. I wouldn't be the person I am today without you in my life. Thank you for your unconditional love and amazing food over the years (especially the Yorkshire Puddings).

**To my brothers.** Thank you for teaching me how to look after myself when we were younger! You toughened me up and made sure I could stand on my own two feet. Thank you for all the laughs, fun and crazy experiences we have shared and all the fantastic growing up memories. I am excited to be making many more with you.

**To AJ and Georgia**. Thank you for all your smiles, cuddles and fun times. I am really looking forward to many great growing up years with you.

**To Ruth and Dani.** For being there when the going got tough, encouraging me to follow my dream and for never doubting me. I am truly blessed to have you in my life. You are fab and I couldn't ask for better friends.

**To all my extended family and friends.** The experiences and times we have shared have helped me to write this book and be who I am today. Special thanks to Liz and Cliff for all your unconditional love and support. It means the world to me. Lynette – for all the laughs and love along the way. Joph - for your friendship, love and great memories.

**To my Pride team.** For helping me to grow and develop into the person I want to be. I have learnt so much from all of you – personally and professionally. Thank you for sharing so openly and honestly and supporting me with all my ideas (even the far out ones!)

**To my 'Gina' team.** Wow! Look at what we created! Thank you for all your hard work, patience, knowledge and skills. Special thanks to my amazing friend and photographer – Stephen Smart, John Polley for the fabulous graphics and Dom Wint for pulling it all together online for me.

**To all those who I hold close in my heart that have passed over.** Thank you for all the great memories and the time we shared. You continue to inspire me every day. I know you are around me and I thank you for watching over me and the family. Thank you for showing me the way. I love you.

**Lastly, to Paula.** Meeting you was the very best moment of my life. Since starting on our journey together all those years ago, I knew this was going to be perfect. You are my light when it goes dark, you are my guide when I can't see and you are my inspiration always. I am so proud of you and all that you have achieved. Thank you for always being there and for being you. I couldn't wish for any more. Ready for the next phase? xxx

# Introduction: How to Use This Book

It is not enough to just read this book.

Reading it will only put the ideas in your head and soon after you will forget the principles.

It is like when you attend a training course at school or at work. You are engaged, empowered, motivated and learning whilst you are in the room. When you get back to the office or classroom you file the notes and soon after you have forgotten all about what you have learned or even heard in that room. Then when you have a clear out of your space, you find the notes and think back to the training. You remember how good the day was but have forgotten all the details about it. Does this sound familiar?

Within the covers of this book, you will find tips and strategies that you can introduce straight away into your life. These tips will help you to become a happier and healthier person and to feel on top of your game. You will also find summaries (to remind you of the key points), to do lists, questions to think about, exercises and quizzes throughout to really get you thinking about what you do now and how you can make some simple changes.

The book is split into four sections: food, exercise, stress and spirit. We will look at a wide range of aspects around food and how to eat well for optimum health and performance.
We will look at exercise and how to become more active day to day. We will then look at stress, the impact it can have on your health and ways to minimise the stress in your life. We will finish by looking at ways to nourish your spirit and how to live in spirit every day. We also talk about balance and how to achieve balance in your daily life.

All of what you read here are things that I have learnt over the years and I apply every day. I only talk to you about the things I do myself and explain the benefits I have seen as a result.

In 2007 I was diagnosed with IBS (irritable bowel syndrome). The diagnosis was vague and I wasn't offered any support or information on what I could do to help alleviate my symptoms. It was at this point that I decided I needed to learn how to manage my symptoms without reliance on medication. I introduced small changes gradually to my diet, lifestyle and outlook on life. I share with you the ideas and principles I have learnt along the way. All of these things have enabled me to live symptom free from IBS. The knowledge I share with you here has come to me through reading books, from the internet and conversations with people about their experiences. I am totally self-taught and as a result I am not blinded by the science and technicalities behind it all. I will tell you what I know and give you ideas on how you can start to introduce these principles into your life.

I will keep everything as straight forward as possible, without much technical language or science. That way, you can really enjoy reading about the principles and strategies and can start to change things today, without a dictionary in hand.

So remember, if you don't use it, you will lose it. Be proactive with your learning. Make notes, talk to people about it and practice the principles every day until they become a habit for you.

You need to be willing to learn from what you read and take action upon it. I suggest you read this book with a pencil in your hand and have somewhere handy to take notes.

You will come across something in the book that you want to try out. You will also come across some of the things that you already do. You will, hopefully, start to think in a different way and have your eyes opened to how powerful the elements discussed in the book are for achieving a fully functioning, energetic body and mind.

Start to try the things out that you identify with. See how they make you feel, act and be as a result. Note any changes that you become aware of. Speak to others to see if they notice a difference in you.

The principles in the book are for the long haul, not a short-term fix. If you really want to be the best you can be and get the most out of your life and your body, start off by understanding the principles. Then look at the importance of each one and start to incorporate them into your life on a daily basis. Don't give up at the first hurdle. Persevere and see the difference it can make to your life.

So, don't just read this book. Really embrace it. Take on board the principles and start to live a healthier and more productive life. Work at being the best that you can be. The principles really are that powerful.

So, let us get started. Grab yourself a pen and paper and let us get moving on the journey towards achieving your perfect health.

# Part 1:
# Everything You Need to Know About Nutrition

# Section 1: The Basics

## Chapter 1: Introduction to Food

Food. We all eat it. We all have to eat. Everyone has a different response to it. Some people like tomatoes. Some don't (me included). Some people like avocados. Others think they resemble the green slime from Ghostbusters and despise them. Some people like marmite. Others grimace at the thought of it.

Food is essential to life. Food gives us the nutrients and energy our body needs to maintain health and life. It is needed to grow and develop, to work, to play, to move, to think and to learn. Without it, you will die. It really is that simple.

We all have different experiences, habits and thoughts of food. Some people eat it for comfort and some people eat it for fuel. Some people enjoy eating and others don't. I'm sure you will know someone that fits into each of those categories. Most of our habits were formed in childhood and stay with us long into adulthood. Some of these habits are good and some are not so good.

Food provides fuel for the body. It is what keeps you going throughout the day and gives you all the energy you need to function.

Think back to a time when you didn't eat all day. How did you feel? Were you tired, nauseous and lacking in energy? Were you irritable, snappy and on edge? I know that I resemble a little monster when I don't eat! Now think back to a time when you were eating healthy foods all day, including snacks and meals. How did you feel then? Did you have lots of energy, a positive frame of mind and were you focused?

Did you have a productive day, get on well with people and feel good? It is great to feel like this, isn't it?

The food you eat has a massive impact on how your body functions and the output you can expect from it. It also affects your mood and frame of mind.

How you treat your body affects what you will get out of it. Imagine you eat the same things every day. This consists of burgers, chips, microwave meals, crisps and chocolate. How does this make you feel? I am pretty sure you will feel sluggish and run down after a while. You are putting limited nutrients in to your body and as a result you will be running mainly on sugar and fat.

Now imagine you put in lots of fresh fruit and vegetables, good quality proteins, essential fats and carbohydrates. (Don't worry if this means nothing to you right now. I will explain what these are later on.) You vary the food that you are putting in every day. Your body is nourished and you feel good. It is getting lots of vitamins and minerals and is able to function fully. It gives you all the energy you need and you perform at 100% all day.

Let us think for a moment about actual foods you eat and what is going on in the body to reiterate this point. Imagine you eat a healthy grilled chicken salad with olive oil drizzled over the top. There are nuts and seeds sprinkled over it too. You are giving your body a healthy meal that is packed with vitamins and minerals, carbohydrates, protein and essential fats.

Here, you are feeding your cells healthy foods, which in turn will produce healthy tissues, healthy organs, healthy systems and a healthy body.

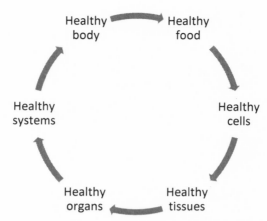

Now imagine you are eating a hamburger and chips from one of the leading fast food specialists. The burgers are generally served on white bread, the meat is processed and the chips are covered in salt. The nutrients you put into your body here are limited and not of good quality. The food is processed, contains sugar, salt and saturated fats.

This time around you are putting in unhealthy foods. This will, in turn, produce unhealthy cells, unhealthy tissues, unhealthy organs, unhealthy systems and the end result will be an unhealthy body.

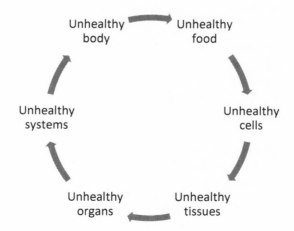

The wrong chemicals enter the body when you feed yourself the incorrect or bad foods. This will result in health issues and complications with the effective running of the body.

Optimum health begins with what you eat and the chain of events starts off at a cellular level, as I just mentioned. You are in control of what you eat and therefore in total control of your health. You. Not your partner, your mum and dad, your brother, sister or your friends. No one forces you to eat what you do. You alone choose what you put in and the results you can expect to see. If you don't put the best fuel in, how can you expect your body to work for you 24 hours a day and give you all the energy you need?

Start to think of food as sacred. It is not there just to provide energy. It is there to nourish your body and cells so you can be, do and achieve anything you want. You need to make sure you are nourishing your body in the right way with the right things.

Food has its own energy and should be treated with respect. You should be aware of how different foods affect you physically and mentally. Really give some thought about how different foods make you feel and the energy of what you take into your body.

This book is here to start you on that journey and to piece together how to achieve a healthy body and mind, for life.

## Summary

- Being the best you can be starts with giving your body the best fuel and nourishment you can.
- You are responsible for your own health.
- If you want to be healthy and perform to the best of your ability, start by looking at what you eat.

# Chapter 2: When to Eat and How to Eat

There are two things you need to get right above all else when it comes to food. These are 'when to eat' and 'how to eat'. Once you have this in hand, you can start to make simple tweaks to the foods you eat.

Let us look at the key points about when to eat and how to eat first. Then we will delve into the nitty gritty of the foods which will nourish you and help you to feel on top of your game.

**When to Eat**

Ok, so when you eat. It is really important to think about this.

Imagine getting in late from work and feeling very hungry. When you are so hungry, you will probably grab the first thing you can find. This may be unhealthy foods, such as biscuits, chocolate bars or something that takes only 3 minutes to cook in the microwave. You eat, drink and then, since it is so late, you go straight to bed.

Is this the best thing to be putting into your body late at night and just before you sleep? You are putting in lots of sugar, calories and fat. You are inactive after this point so the food is not burned off. Over time, if you continue to do this, your body will crave food at this late hour and you will find weight starts to creep on to your body.

So why is timing of eating important? Here are three reasons.

1. If you feed your body at regular intervals, you will have more sustained energy throughout the day.
2. If you eat the right things at the right times in the day, you can expect to maintain a stable and sustainable weight.

3.  It will maintain your focus and concentration as well as your metabolism all through the day. It will also maintain your blood sugar levels throughout the day. This will ensure you don't keep thinking about reaching for that chocolate bar in the cupboard or those amazing biscuits in the round tin at around the mid-morning or mid-afternoon mark.

It can be very tricky to eat regularly. It can also be a cause of some amusement for others. Finding time to eat and look after yourself, for some, is not as important as all the other things going on in their day to day lives. For others, it is THE most important thing.

I used to be someone who got on with life and ate when I really needed to. I could be found reaching for the chocolate bars, fast food or chips late at night. I would skip breakfast and lunch and look forward to my late evening meal. I felt tired, run down and pretty rubbish most of the time. Now, I fit everything else around my eating! I don't schedule anything in at breakfast, lunch or evening meal times. I always have food with me and make sure I eat every few hours. I have come to learn that my body needs good food to do everything I want it to do. I listen to it and respond by giving it the things that will nourish it. I feel great as a result. I aim to talk to you about all the things I do that can help you to feel the same.

Without your health and wellness, you would be unable to tackle any of the things going on in your life. So make it a priority.

I struggle some days to find time to eat. However, if I don't, I feel a slump in energy. Sometimes this is experienced at the time when I can't eat. Other times this is the day after, when not eating properly the day before catches up with me. It isn't easy to find time when you are busy. I can guarantee that you will feel the effects of it if you don't. .

Your health is the one thing you have ultimate control over. As such, make sure you schedule in time to eat to nourish your body. Avoid booking yourself up over lunchtime or evening meals. Be in control of your diary and make sure you keep hold of it. Learn to say no to people.

I take food with me everywhere. I am never found without some food in my bag. The reason? I want to make sure that I am performing at my best all day and have all the energy I need to complete my tasks and activities.

When I worked within education, the first thing that my colleagues observed when I headed in to the office was me pulling out a mountain of food from my bag. They would look at what I pulled out and comment on it. For a typical day at work I would take with me a selection of seasonal fruit, a selection of nuts and seeds, a fruit smoothie, crackerbreads with some form of dip, a big bottle of water (which I refill throughout the day) and a tub packed full of salad with some meat. At strategic points during the day I would be found eating some of the delights I had with me. Comments would fly around about the amount I eat and how often. Without fail, my colleagues would be found fighting over the round biscuit tin in the cupboard at around 10.30-11am and 2.30-3pm. Every day. I was happy with the knowledge I had eaten really well all day and still had the energy to go home and do more. My colleagues were generally flagging, grumpy and hungry at home time. This is what I call the 'biscuit tin blues.' They would often say they wish they could be more like me. With a little forward planning and will power, they could!

When you eat has a massive impact on your body and performance. Try out these tips to take back control of your eating.

Make sure you eat when you are hungry. Your body will give you the signal when you are hungry. So eat! Don't ignore it. It is so easy to get busy and to either a. forget to eat, b. pretend you aren't hungry and ignore it or c. blatantly ignore your stomach shouting at you. It is shouting for a reason! Have you ever ignored it and got to the point of feeling sick and faint? Then wanted to eat anything and everything in sight? Usually reaching for something sweet? Because you waited until you HAD to eat, your blood sugar levels dipped. There is no time to cook, plan or even think straight when you reach this stage. Anything in sight will be consumed, just short of the dog. Listen to your body, get to know the signs it gives you and then act. You will start to recognise the subtle signs from your body that will indicate when you are hungry.

I know I am hungry when my stomach starts grumbling a little. I start to feel a little light headed and irritable with myself, especially if I am in the middle of something and not wanting to break off from it. I recognise the hunger signs very quickly these days and always have something close to hand, be it on my desk or in my bag. As soon as I eat, I feel much better and I regain my focus. What are the signs you notice when you are hungry?

Aim to eat regularly throughout the day. Space out your meals and snacks and have them at regular intervals. I usually find I am hungry after 2 - 3 hours. I always eat something at this time. Recognise the times when you feel hungry and plan to eat then.

Planning ahead is the key to eating well throughout the day. I will talk about planning ahead in 'how to eat'.

Eat three main meals a day. Try to space these out with snacks in between. If you eat snacks, you will generally eat less at meal times. Your hunger will be reduced because your blood sugar levels are balanced.

Breakfast is a meal that is generally overlooked. Some people really struggle to eat as soon as they are up and moving about. Others are so hungry they could eat a horse. I always recommend eating or drinking something within half an hour of waking. If you do this, it will kick start your metabolism.

Without food in your belly, you will be running on empty and your body will hold on to food and energy to preserve itself. If you feed it, your body thinks you are going to keep feeding it, so it will start to wake up. If you don't, your body will go into the starvation mode. This is where the body holds on to everything it has within it in the attempt to protect itself for a famine.

For some, breakfast is really difficult. Most of the time it is not that they can't eat. It is that they have formed a habit and the body has become used to it. Then when they try to eat breakfast, they feel unwell and remind themselves 'this is why I don't eat breakfast'. They give up after only a few days of trying. If this is you, think about this. If you can remember, think about the time when you started to not eat breakfast. At first it will have been a struggle and your body will have been screaming out for food. With enough ignoring of these screams, your body will have become used to not having food in the morning. It will have taken some time for your body to adjust to this new pattern. Does this sound familiar? Train your body to expect food regularly. It takes 21 days to form a new habit. Start today on the journey to changing the breakfast habit.

Snacks. Try to eat a mid-morning and mid-afternoon snack every day. This will maintain your blood sugar levels and provide energy at regular points throughout the day. Without snacks, you will find your energy levels reduce and you reach for something sweet in response. You want to aim to keep your snacks small enough so they are not a main meal but large enough to keep you going for a few hours.

Snacks are great. They are an opportunity for you to eat different combinations of foods to really spice up your daily eating. I love having a wide range of choice for snacks. I find that I am very creative with combinations! I talk about snacks, both good and bad, further on in the book, so if you are looking for ideas, take a look there.

## How to Eat

How to eat. Sounds silly doesn't it? It may do to you right now but it is a really important element to consider when thinking about being the best you can be. Let us spend some time thinking about this.

Do you 'just' eat? By that I mean, you make something and sit and eat it with no distractions. With a knife and fork, from plate to mouth. Just concentrating on eating what you have in front of you and nothing else.

Do you stand and eat? Maybe you walk and eat? Or do you sit and eat at a table?

Do you ever think about how you actually eat?

Most people don't think about these things at all. Eating is something that just happens when they have food in front of them.

I want us to think for a moment about someone that is clinically thought of as morbidly obese. Do you think they sit and think about how they eat? Do you think they consider what they eat? Do you think eating is just a habit for them? Now think of someone that is in the normal range of weight. Ask yourself the same questions. Are there any discrepancies in the answer? No?

Eating is something we are taught to do from an early age. The physical action of eating is ingrained into our motor functions. Just like the process and formation of words with a pen is.

For a moment, sit and think about the physical skills you need to feed yourself. The plate of food is prepared for you and you are sitting at the table. How would you physically eat the food?

Most people in the western world would pick up the knife and fork. You would need to have spatial awareness to reach the knife and fork and you would contract your muscles in the fingers and hand to pick them up. You would then need to move the knife and fork, maybe cutting or separating food on the plate, and coordinate them together to enable you to pick up food off the plate. You would then need to have spatial awareness and coordination skills to navigate the fork to your mouth. Once the food is in your mouth, your hand would find its way naturally back to the plate. Your mouth would start to work to chew and swallow the food. Now think about this. Have you considered that process while eating? Or ever? There is a skill to eating and feeding yourself that most of us take for granted.

Do you see now that how you eat will affect your overall performance and wellbeing?

Let us look now at how to eat. Here are a few ideas and strategies that will start you off in the right direction.

Turn the TV off and get rid of any distractions. Really concentrate on the food and eating it. If you do this, you will be fully present in the experience. If you are distracted, you will be less aware of the amount and quality of the food you are consuming. Think about when you last sat in front of the TV and ate. What do you remember about that meal? Was it how it tasted or was it the storyline that was unfolding before your eyes?

Just as you took the time out to read the paragraph above and you visualised the process of eating, take the time to eat consciously. Look at what you are eating. Smell what you are eating. Think about how it looks, smells and tastes with every mouthful. Really engage the senses in what you eat. Enjoy every mouthful. This will give you a fuller and richer experience of the food you eat and you will start to look forward to mealtimes.

Slow down when you eat. If you engage all the senses as described above, this will help to slow you down. After every mouthful, place your knife and fork down on the table. Slowing down will enable your mind to catch up with your belly! The message from your belly to your mind is a little slower than most people would like.

Think back to a time when you went out for a meal and you ate all the food on your plate. You felt full to busting. Then after 20 minutes or so, you felt painfully full, uncomfortable and groggy. The message from your belly to your mind came later. You could have stopped a few forkfuls from the end of the meal. But you thought you had more room so it was squished in. You really didn't need the last few fork loads. Slowing down will enable you to hear the messages when you are actually full.

Give yourself enough time to eat. If you rush, the message of fullness will be delayed and you could overeat. You will probably also get indigestion from eating quickly and rushing to get on with other things.

Sit and eat. If you stand and eat or walk and eat, your body won't digest the food as well. Sitting enables your body to concentrate on processing the food you are feeding it. It doesn't need to think about any other processes and can fully concentrate its efforts on digestion. If you walk, your body will get confused and not know whether to digest or concentrate its efforts on the physical movement.

Stop when you think you are full. If you think you are full, you more than likely are! A good thought is to feed your body to 80% fullness. This will ensure you are not overeating and will enable your mind to catch up with your belly. Don't try to fit a little bit extra in or to finish what is on your plate. Stop when you start to feel full.

Chew every mouthful with care and fully. This will enable digestion to occur much easier and without as much effort.

Eat when you are hungry, as mentioned in 'when to eat'. This will ensure you are maintaining your blood sugar levels and feeding your body when it asks for it. You will notice an increase in your energy levels and concentration as a result.

Plan ahead. If you know you are going into work all day and only have vending machines stacked with unhealthy sweets and treats, why not prepare something to take with you instead? Prepare your breakfast, your mid-morning snack, your lunch, your mid-afternoon snack and your dinner if you need to. Prepare it all the night before if you know you won't get time in the morning. Put it in tubs/containers/bags and place it in the fridge to keep it fresh. Then in the morning, you can just take it out of the fridge, put it in your bag and head off for a day at work. You know then that you have all the food you need for the day, without having to nip to the vending machine or shop where you may make more unhealthy choices.

I like the Pareto Rule and apply it to my eating all the time. I call it the 80-20 rule. I eat 80% healthily throughout the week and 20% of whatever I would like. This includes treats. The 80% incorporates all the good things you will read further in the book. As I eat 80% healthily throughout the week, I have found that the 20% is usually less than 20% at the end of the week. The treats I allow myself, I tend not to fancy when it comes down to it because I can see and feel the difference the sugar and fat makes in my body. I start to feel sluggish after the treats and crave more of them the next day. This only happens after these treats. I still like them but, as I eat well the majority of the time and I exercise and keep active in the week, the treats have started to take the form of healthier versions.

So the key to remember, eat 80% healthily and allow 20% treats. This will ensure the food you eat and the lifestyle you follow will be sustainable. If you don't allow yourself that square of chocolate (or whatever your treat might be) you will crave it. Every waking hour will be consumed with thoughts of that square of chocolate. Allow yourself the flexibility to eat it and your mind will not focus on it.

## Over to You

Do you do any of these strategies now? If not, which ones could you try out to improve your eating habits? Make a plan of which you will try out so you can take back control of your eating.

Notice how various foods make you feel differently. Identify the foods that make you feel great and give you lots of sustained energy. Identify the foods that make you feel sluggish and tired. Make a note these and incorporate more of the good foods and less of the ones that don't feel so good. Some foods will make you feel better than others. These will be different from your friends, family and colleagues. We are all different and react differently to the various foods. Take note of which ones are good for you.

## Summary

- When you eat is a major consideration to being the best that you can be.
- Make time to eat and nourish your body.
- Prioritise eating and drinking.
- Eat when you are hungry.
- Eat regularly.
- Aim for three meals and two snacks every day.
- Always eat breakfast. If you aren't a breakfast person, change the habit.
- How you eat impacts hugely on getting the best performance from your body.
- Get rid of distractions while eating.
- Eat consciously.
- Slow down when you eat.
- Give yourself enough time to eat.
- Sit and eat.
- Stop when you are 80% full.
- Chew fully.
- Plan ahead.
- Aim for 80% healthy foods and 20% treats.
- Notice how different foods make you feel.

# Chapter 3: Limiting Beliefs and Habits

### What is a Limiting Belief?

These are the things that you believe about yourself that stop you from doing or being who or what you want to be. Lots of people have limiting beliefs about food, weight and eating, amongst a lot of other things.

Here are a few common ones I have come across about losing weight:

- Losing weight is hard work.
- I can't lose weight unless I… (give up sweets/exercise for at least an hour a day).
- I can't lose weight easily because I have a slow metabolism.
- I must follow a strict diet plan to lose weight.
- My weight isn't that bad, yet.

Other food related beliefs:

- Eating healthily is expensive.
- Food is the only thing that makes me feel better when I am feeling bad.
- I don't have enough time.
- I don't have the willpower.
- Food helps me relax and feel good.

## Over to You

Think now about any beliefs you have that are stopping you from achieving your goals. Make a note of these.

Now ask yourself the following questions:

- Where did this belief come from?
- Who gave me this belief?

- How do I feel about the person that gave me this belief? Do I respect them? Are they always right?
- What is this belief costing me on a daily basis?
- What will holding onto this belief mean for me in the long term?
- How will my life be different if I let go of this belief?
- Am I ready to let go of the belief?

When you step through these questions, you challenge the unhelpful and limiting beliefs that you have acquired. Some of these will have been with you since a child, others may be more recent.

If you are ready to let go of the beliefs, think of the opposite belief to the one you hold. Reframe the limiting belief into a positive one. This way you are replacing it with a helpful and motivating belief. Recite these daily as affirmations so they can become ingrained into your subconscious mind.

For example:
- I struggle with my weight = I am in control of my weight and health.
- Food is the only thing that makes me feel better when I am feeling bad = my body is a reflection of how I view myself and my life.
- I don't have enough time = I give myself the time to eat well for my health and wellbeing.
- Food helps me relax and feel good = food is nourishment.

Only when you have a healthy attitude to food will you be truly in control of your eating. When you have full control over your eating, you will be on the way to being the best you can be. Holding onto limiting beliefs will hold you back from being the best you. So take back that control and really think about the beliefs you hold.

**Habits**

We all have them. Some are good habits and some are not so good.

Do you:
- Always reach for chocolate after a meal?
- Have a slice of cake with your latte?
- Eat a banana every day for breakfast?
- Only eat takeaway on a certain night?

Rest assured, you are not alone!

Habits are developed over time. They do not come on overnight. It takes approximately 21 days to form a new habit. Habits are formed over time, from repetition. All habits can be broken and replaced by new ones.

Take the time now to think of all the things that you do every day. For example, brush your teeth, eat lunch at a certain time or shower at a certain time of day. Make a note of these. Take a look over the list and think about when these were formed, who was involved and how long they took to become ingrained into your life.

There are a number of food related habits that I have come across when working with clients. The most frequent ones are listed below.

**Cravings.** Most people don't realise they are craving something until they raise their awareness about their eating habits. Once you learn what the craving is, you can then develop a strategy to control it. A good example of a craving is wanting to eat chocolate after all meals. A possible strategy to control this is to wait 20 minutes after eating and then decide if you still want it.

**Clean the plate.** This is a habit formed in childhood (generally). I remember eating with my Grandma and Grandad and them always saying, 'you are not leaving the table until you have cleared your plate'. My brothers and I would sit there until the plate was clear. My mum always said the same, especially with Sunday Lunch. This passes through generations – my brother now says this to his young son. It is almost as if you can't be full until you have eaten everything on that plate. A young child may say they are full and know that they are. The parent thinks they know best and tells them to eat up, even though the child knows they are full. Now imagine you have two different sized plates – one little and one large. You can fit different size portions on each plate, right? If you have the 'clean the plate' habit, consider eating off smaller plates.

**Watching TV while eating.** This encourages eating more than you need to. You are distracted and not fully present in the moment. As a result, you are not aware of how full you are.

Other common habits:
- Eating too fast.
- Eating when you're not hungry.
- Eating when standing up.
- Always eating dessert after the evening meal.
- Skipping meals.

## Over to You

Do you know what your food habits are?

Think about keeping a food diary. Keep an in-depth diary of all the foods and drinks that you consume in the week, complete with times of day and exercise routines. Keeping a diary will help you to identify the habits that you have.

I routinely ask clients to detail verbally what they eat in a week. It is surprising (to them) that what they tell me they eat and what they actually eat, is usually quite different. It is easy to forget about the sneaky biscuit you ate at 10.30, that 3rd cup of coffee in the morning meeting, the bit of chocolate after dinner or that 4th glass of wine that poured itself. When you write down what you actually eat in a day and week, it highlights the habits, the patterns and the cravings that you are having. Armed with this information, you can then minimise or cut the cravings and form new, healthier habits.

Think of all the food-related habits you have that are harmful to you; your mind, your body and your soul. Write these down. Keeping the food diary will help with this.

Identify the triggers for the unhealthy behaviours. What are the things that will 'make' you want to eat unhealthily? Is it the 3rd glass of wine that makes you reach for the crisps?

Identify a couple of habits that you want to work on. Think about the triggers that lead up to it and how you know you will fall into the habit.

For example:
- Walking in to the staff room and seeing the open biscuit tin.
- Leaving work late and not knowing what is for dinner.
- Being offered a chocolate or slice of cake when it is a colleague's birthday in the office.

Consider what you could do to avoid or minimise these triggers and make an action plan. For example, in team meetings I offer to take water in instead of making everyone coffee. I will bring fruit in instead of a box of chocolates.

Replace your unhealthy habits with new, healthy ones. What could you do differently? What could you eat instead or what could you do to create healthy opportunities? This could be planning meals the day before or eating only when you are hungry.

If you know that you eat too quickly when alone, think about arranging to eat with colleagues, family, friends as often as you can.

Reinforce these new habits. If you find you slip back into the old habit, stop yourself as soon as you realise. Ask yourself why this happened and how you can ensure this doesn't happen again. Don't give yourself a hard time if you do slip. Remember a new habit takes 21 days to form and to break an old one. The new habit won't be ingrained overnight. Be patient and kind to yourself. Take one day at a time and celebrate your successes on your journey.

## Addictions

What is an addiction? Dependence means feeling that you need a substance in order to carry on doing what you want to do, even if problems result from its use. If you are dependent on a substance then you might be said to be addicted to it.

There are many types of addiction. The most commonly discussed ones are alcohol, drugs, smoking, gambling, sex and shopping. Some are more harmful than others, to yourself but also to others around you.

## How Addictions Start

It starts with a first 'go' or try of something. This could be to experiment to see what the substance is like. Once you have tried it, you may use the substance again. Then you may begin to use it on an occasional basis. Something might happen and you begin to use it on a more regular basis. Then you may find it difficult to stop. Your body feels like it NEEDS it to survive. The amount consumed may also begin to increase over time. For some substances, the body rapidly becomes tolerant of a dose taken and the user will increase the amount to achieve a desired effect.

Most addictions take time to develop and almost no one deliberately sets out to become addicted to a substance.

You can't be in the best physical or mental health if you are addicted to a substance. The substance takes control of you and will affect your health. You need to deal with any addictions before you can start to think about achieving optimum physical and mental wellbeing.

If you have an addiction, deal with this first. Only when you have dealt with this can you be in total control of your body and mind.

**Is it a Habit or an Addiction?**
Think about the following questions.

- Do you NEED to have it? (addiction)
- Do you CHOOSE to have it? (habit)

If it is a habit, what could you do now to break this habit?

If it is an addiction, are you ready to break the addiction? There is a wide range of advice, treatment and support services for addiction in the UK, which anyone with a substance-related problem should have access to. Ask your GP for details. You could also look for community support groups in your local area. Most local community drug units also run drop-in centres, which don't require a referral from a doctor. You should be able to find information about these on the internet or ask at your doctors' surgery. There is a wealth of help out there for you when you are ready to make changes.

## Summary

- ♥ Be in control of your mind and challenge the limiting beliefs you hold.
- ♥ Holding onto them will restrict you from being the best you can be.
- ♥ Identify the limiting beliefs you have.
- ♥ Challenge these and decide if you are ready to let go.
- ♥ Reframe your negative beliefs into positive, motivating statements.
- ♥ Turn these into affirmations and recite daily.
- ♥ Keep a food diary to clearly see your habits and cravings.
- ♥ Break old, unhealthy habits and replace with new, healthy ones.
- ♥ Be patient and kind to yourself.
- ♥ New habits don't become ingrained overnight.
- ♥ Break any addictions to achieve peak physical and mental health.

# Chapter 4: Barriers to Eating Well

What is it that stops you from eating well?

- No time
- Lack of support or buy in from loved ones
- Having to make 3 versions of dinner – yours, your partner's and your children's
- Eating healthily costs more
- Bad habits
- Too much contrasting information is available
- A love of eating out

These are the main barriers clients highlight to me.

## Over to You

Think for a moment now about your barriers. Write down all of the barriers you have to eating well. Be honest and accurate in what you write down.

Do you think any of these ACTUALLY stop you from eating healthily? Are these actual barriers or perceived barriers? Are you using one or more of these to not make the changes in your lifestyle? After all, it won't be easy to make the changes. Will it?

Look over this list and categorise it into two: actual barriers and perceived barriers.

Out of the list we are going to look at the actual barriers.

The actual barriers are the ones that stop you from achieving the healthy, balanced eating that you desire.

Now, take each one in turn and think about where this barrier has come from. Is it your barrier, your mum's, your partner's, your grandparents'?

Does holding on to the thought of it actually help you in anyway? If not, are you ready to leave it behind and to think about how to move around it?

If you are ready, think of at least three ways you can make the barrier smaller or non-existent. For example, if you hold the barrier, 'I have no time to eat healthy':

1. Prepare lunch the night before (instead of watching the news) and put it in the fridge – no need to buy food whilst at work.
2. Plan ahead. When going shopping plan the week's meals (roughly) so you know the ingredients you need to buy.
3. Buy fruit, nuts, seeds and crackers. These are easy to put in your bag as a snack.

Get the idea? Once you have done this for all the barriers you have, you will have some ideas of how to start to eat healthier. Then you need to implement them!

## Summary

- List your barriers.
- Are you ready to move around them?
- If so, take each barrier in turn and list 3 ways you can make it smaller or non-existent.
- Start to implement the ideas!

# Chapter 5: Impact of Not Eating Well

Food is fuel. Without food you would not be alive. We all need food.

You have a choice over the foods you eat. As we have already explored, the foods you choose will affect how you feel and will directly impact on your health and wellbeing.

It is well known that the following health issues and diseases have a root cause or risk factor associated with food and diet.

- Obesity
- Heart disease
- Stroke
- Some cancers
- Metabolic syndrome (a collection of symptoms that can lead to heart disease and diabetes)
- Diabetes
- Hypertension (high blood pressure)
- High cholesterol
- Asthma
- Some types of arthritis
- Menstrual irregularities
- Infertility
- Eczema

If you could choose, would you rather be fit and healthy or have one or a combination of the above issues?

I can only assume that you would want the first option.

Just as you can choose whether you want to be fit and healthy or not, you have a choice of what you put in to your body. If you choose fit and healthy, follow the guidance in the book.

If you want to be ill and lack energy, be irritable and feel run down, choose to ignore everything in this book. The choice is yours. Only you are responsible for your body and health.

Let us look for a moment at some of the common illnesses and diseases and the dietary reasons why these occur, according to medical research. Knowledge is power after all.

**Coronary heart disease.** There is an increased risk of this when you eat a diet high in fat (particularly saturated fat) and high in salt.

**Cancer.** A third of cancers can be prevented by changes to the diet. A diet high in fibre and whole grain cereal and low in fat has the potential to prevent a number of cancers, including colon, stomach and breast cancer.

**Obesity.** A diet high in fat, sugar and salt leads to weight gain and increases the risk of obesity. This is true for both children and adults. Carrying excessive weight doesn't just increase the risk of heart disease, diabetes, cancer and infertility. It can also result in fatigue, low self-esteem and poor mental and physical performance.

**Additives, preservatives and refined sugar.** A diet high in these can cause poor concentration, hyperactivity and aggression. Foods high in sugar and additives lack the mineral chromium. Chromium is needed in the body to metabolise fats and carbohydrates and to break down insulin. It helps to control blood sugar levels. If these are out of balance, it can trigger behavioural problems.

**Fertility issues.** An unhealthy diet that is high in fat, sugar and processed foods and low in the nutrients that are essential to fertility can lead to infertility and increase the chances of miscarriage.

**Calcium.** A diet low in the mineral calcium increases the risk of bones becoming weak or brittle. This is a condition known as osteoporosis.

**Depression and mood swings**. An unhealthy diet increases the risk of depression and mood swings.

**High in sugar.** A diet too high in sugar can lead to too much glucose (a form of sugar carried in the bloodstream) circulating in your body. Too much glucose in the blood indicates development of blood sugar problems, such as diabetes. Look out for an increase in thirst, a frequent need to urinate and problems with vision, fatigue and recurrent infections.

**Immune system.** Eating an unhealthy diet can put a strain on the immune system. Have you ever noticed when you don't eat fruit and vegetables that you become run down and end up with a cold, flu or cold sores? A balanced intake of the essential vitamins and minerals will strengthen the immune system, ensure it works correctly and provide protection from infections and diseases.

An unhealthy diet is also linked to premenstrual syndrome, food cravings and anxiety amongst many other things.

## Summary

- An unhealthy diet results in health issues, complications and disease.
- You can choose whether you are in full health or have health issues.
- What you eat is the key to how you feel and perform.
- The food you choose to eat will directly influence your health.

## Summary Section 1

So far we have looked at the basics of eating well.

Below I detail the key things to be thinking about around this and things that you can start doing right now.

I have also listed the exercises I mentioned throughout the section to remind you of activities that can help you around eating well.

## To-Do List

- Think about when you eat. What could you tweak around this to make sure you are eating regularly? What are your triggers to unhealthy eating? What could you do to minimise these?
- Think about how you eat. What could you do to make sure you are more present when eating? What are your triggers to eating badly? What could you to do lessen these times?
- Plan your meals and snacks loosely for the week.

## The Listed Exercises

- How do different foods make you feel?
- Sensory exploration of a meal. Really taste, feel and smell every mouthful.
- Challenge your beliefs. Turn your limiting beliefs into positive affirmations that you repeat daily.
- Explore your habits and triggers. Action plan to minimise the unhealthy ones.
- Keep a food diary to help identify habits and patterns.
- Identify your barriers to eating well and plan how you can get around these barriers.

# Section 2: Eating Healthily

## Chapter 6: What to Eat

In the following section you will find information on:

- Carbohydrates
- The Glycaemic Index
- Protein
- Fat
- Vitamins and minerals
- Drinks
- Balancing the diet
- Ideas for meals

I have tried to keep the science to a minimum but it is needed at points to understand what is going on in the body and why our bodies respond in certain ways. Don't worry if it doesn't all make sense at this stage. Take on board the practical tips and make sure you know the things you should be eating and the things you should be leaving well alone.

When you have read the section and understand it, work to spread the word. Educate all those around you: your family members, friends, children, colleagues and acquaintances. Help them to understand the basics, which will in turn help them to adopt healthier eating habits and enable them to reach optimum performance too.

Only when you can control what you put in, will you be able to control what you get out. When you can fully control your hand to mouth action can you truly be the best you can be. This section will give you all the information you need to make sure you are controlling what goes in.

Read on!

## Carbohydrates

Most people know of carbohydrates (or carbs as they are more commonly known) as the nutrient that gives you energy. In this section, we will look at what carbohydrates are, what they are needed for and the different types. We will explore which are the good ones you should be eating and which are the ones you should be staying away from and why. We will also look at the Glycaemic Index and why it is so fundamentally important to understand. So, let's get cracking.

### What are Carbohydrates?
Carbohydrates are one of the three macronutrients. The other two macronutrients are protein and fat. A macronutrient is one that your body needs in larger quantities than the micronutrients (which are the vitamins and minerals).

When you eat carbohydrates, they are digested and used in your body in a range of different ways. They are either used immediately as fuel or sent to your liver or muscles. Some may enter your adipose tissue (fat tissue). We will look at how this happens and why in a few minutes.

### Why Do We Need Carbohydrates?
Your body uses carbohydrates mainly for energy. Some of your body cells, especially in your brain and your red blood cells, prefer to run on glucose. Glucose is a type of sugar that is obtained through the intake of carbohydrates. When you exercise, your muscles can also use glucose as their main source of fuel. 1 gram of carbohydrates gives you 4 calories of energy, just to give you something to think about.

### Structure of Carbohydrates
All carbohydrates are made up of molecules or units called saccharides.

There are 3 basic categories:

1. Simple carbohydrates – also referred to as 'sugar.'
2. Complex carbohydrates – also referred to as 'starches.'
3. Non-starch polysaccharides (NSP) – commonly referred to as 'fibre.'

## Are you ready for the science bit?

### Simple Carbohydrates

Simple carbohydrates have a very basic structure (hence the name) and usually only contain one or two units of sugar made up from a combination of glucose, fructose and galactose. Most people have heard of glucose and fructose since they are commonly found in the ingredients lists of foods.

Single molecules of 'sugars' are known as monosaccharides and consist of either glucose, fructose or galactose.

Two molecules of 'sugars' that are joined together are known as disaccharides.

- When glucose + fructose molecules combine they make sucrose
- When glucose + galactose molecules combine they make lactose
- When glucose + glucose molecules combine they make maltose

Take a look on the back of a food labels and you will see these sugars listed.

Since simple carbohydrates are 'sugars' they are easily and quickly absorbed into your bloodstream for quick energy. They raise your blood sugar levels which give your muscles fuel fast. However, they don't do anything to sustain energy and hunger over longer periods of time. So if you want to have energy or stay full over a longer period of time, don't eat simple carbohydrates!

**What are Classed as Simple Carbohydrates?**
Healthy options for simple carbohydrates:
- Fruit (fructose)
- Some vegetables (maltose)
- Dairy products: milk, yoghurt, cottage cheese (lactose)

Less healthy options:
- Biscuits and cookies
- Sweets, chocolate bars and snack bars
- Crisps
- Soft drinks, carbonated drinks and sports drinks
- Coffee creamers
- Products made with white flour: bread sticks, baked goods, bread, pasta, cakes, pastries, packaged cereals, crackers
- Dips, pre-prepared foods and sauces in jars
- Processed fruit drinks and juices
- Table sugar
- Corn syrup
- Honey, molasses, maple syrup and brown sugar

The less healthy options all contain excessive sugar (higher then 15g per 100g). They also contain processed, low quality fats and have a high energy density. They contain no vitamins or minerals and adversely affect your insulin response, which leads to energy spikes and dips throughout the day. You will notice at one point you have lots of energy and then at another point feel like you need to eat sugar urgently. This is the insulin response in action. We will look at this in more detail in the Glycaemic Index section.

Opt for the healthier versions of simple carbohydrates to stop these energy spikes and dips from taking place throughout the day.

## Are you ready for the science bit?

### Complex Carbohydrates

These consist of many molecules of glucose joined together in long and complicated, branched chains.

The multiple molecules of glucose are called polysaccharides. Once eaten, these polysaccharides are broken down into glucose, absorbed into the bloodstream and either stored or metabolised accordingly. All such carbohydrates will provide energy.

There are 2 types of complex carbohydrates, known as refined and unrefined.

**Refined** carbohydrates have been processed in some way. The processing removes the germ and bran coating from the grain, which strips away the fibre and most of the vitamins.

**Unrefined** is where the grain is left whole. The grains and products are termed whole grain if they haven't been processed in any way. How can you tell if they have been processed? When you look at the ingredients list you should see the first ingredient classed as 'whole-wheat' or 'whole grain'.

Which foods are classed as refined complex carbohydrates?
* White bread
* White pasta
* White rice
* Cakes, biscuits and pastries
* Rice cakes

Which foods are classed as unrefined complex carbohydrates?

- Wholemeal or whole grain products: bread, pasta, rice, noodles
- Fresh and frozen vegetables
- Sweet potatoes
- Yams
- Pulses
- Quinoa

**Why Choose Unrefined over Refined Carbohydrates?**

Refined carbohydrates have been processed. Since they have been stripped of all goodness, they contain virtually no vitamins or minerals and will cause spikes and dips in your energy levels throughout the day. You will feel really hungry and tired at certain points in the day as a result of eating these.

Unrefined carbohydrates are untouched. As a result, they contain all the good stuff they are meant to contain! The vitamins and minerals are intact; they contain antioxidants and phytochemicals, high levels of dietary fibre and traces of amino acids (needed to form proteins). These are definitely the ones you should be choosing. They are the key to balancing your blood sugar levels throughout the day and boosting your energy levels.

# Fibre

Fibre consists of non-starch polysaccharides which is indigestible plant material (such as cellulose, hemicellulose, lignin, pectin, gums and mucilages). Fibre is found in fruits, vegetables, grains and beans. It doesn't provide any energy. Instead, it aids in the transportation of foods through your digestive tract.

There are 2 types of fibre known as insoluble and soluble.

**Insoluble** fibre is normally the outer protective layer of plants. Unrefined wheat, bran, rye, rice and most other grains are primarily composed of insoluble fibre along with fruit and vegetable skins. It bulks out your food and faeces for ease of movement through your digestive tract.

**Soluble** fibre is normally found in the inner part of plants. It can be found in beans, barley, broccoli, prunes, apples, citrus fruits and oats, amongst other foods. It helps with the reduction in cholesterol by binding with the fat in your digestive tract and carrying it all out in the stools.

## Over to You

Take a look at your food intake during the week, looking specifically at your carbohydrate intake. What sources of carbohydrates do you notice? What tweaks can you make to move to the healthier options?

# Summary

How can you use all of this knowledge?

 Know what the difference is between simple, complex, refined and unrefined carbohydrates.

- Eat a variety of simple and complex carbohydrates and fibre in your daily diet.
- Eat whole grain varieties instead of the white, processed versions.
- Eat the healthier simple carbohydrates and limit the unhealthier simple carbohydrates.
- Aim for around 60% of your daily diet to comprise of carbohydrates.

Make these simple changes and you will be off to a great start.

Let us look now at the Glycaemic Index and how this knowledge can help you to boost your energy and to feel great.

# Glycaemic Index

### What is the Glycaemic Index (GI)?

The Glycaemic Index is a ranking of carbohydrate based foods based on their overall effect on blood glucose levels. A foods GI score is based on how quickly it converts carbohydrates to glucose in the body. We are often told to eat low GI foods. But what does this mean and why should we eat the low GI foods?

### The Secret of Glucose and the Glycaemic Index

Your body prefers a specific sugar as its fuel – glucose. Glucose is made after the food you eat has been digested in the stomach. This is then circulated throughout the bloodstream. It is sent to the cells in the body where it is either burned immediately or stored in your liver, muscles and fat stores for later use.

This happens with just about any food that contains carbohydrates. What differs between carbohydrates is how fast the reaction occurs. In very simple terms, the Glycaemic Index is a measure of that speed.

Foods with a high GI score are converted quickly to glucose, while foods with a low GI score are converted more slowly.

If the food you eat is converted too quickly into glucose or you eat lots of food all in one go, the level of glucose will be excess to requirements.

When there is too much glucose circulating in your bloodstream, your body will store some away and release it again when levels are too low. First of all, the body stores it in a base of water known as glycogen, which is held in your liver and muscles. Your glycogen stores have a limit to what they can hold and when they are full, any further excess is stored as fat.

## Summary of the Process

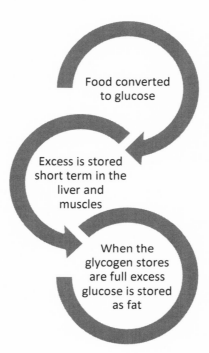

Food converted to glucose

Excess is stored short term in the liver and muscles

When the glycogen stores are full excess glucose is stored as fat

## Frequently Asked Questions

### *How is glucose stored as fat?*

When glucose is released into the bloodstream, it is the job of insulin (a hormone) to take it to where it is needed. If the glucose is released slowly, moderate levels of insulin are released. Your body has time to 'think' about where the glucose is needed the most and will send it there.

If high levels of glucose enter the bloodstream, your body will panic. It might need a certain amount of glucose for fuel at that moment but too much can be harmful. Your body will release high levels of insulin to cope with this and it will store the excess glucose in the liver and muscles (in the glycogen stores). When these are full, the rest will go into your fat stores where it can be stored 'out of the way' and do no harm. This can lead to weight gain if it happens too often.

You need to limit the amount of insulin that is produced in order to discourage fat storage within your body. It is stored in the fat stores until your body needs to convert it back into glucose for energy. You will be aware, I'm sure, that it is much harder to 'lose' the fat store than it is to put it in there in the first place.

Take a look at the graph below. This shows the blood sugar response around eating. The small dotted line is the insulin threshold. If your blood sugar goes above this level it will trigger insulin production and encourage the storage of fat.

The blood sugar levels for a balanced, healthy diet are fairly even throughout the day and shouldn't rise above the insulin threshold. The blood sugar levels for those on an unhealthy diet will rise and dip above and below the line dramatically throughout the day. This will lead to sweet cravings and you will reach for less healthy options as a result. You will also gain weight. Can you identify with the bold line and the energy dips and spikes that happen throughout the day?

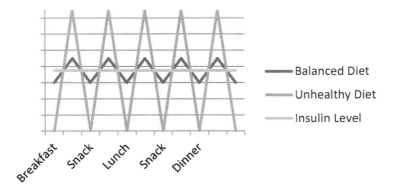

———— Balanced Diet

———— Unhealthy Diet

———— Insulin Level

### *How do I limit insulin production?*

A question that I am often asked!

Choose foods that break down slowly into glucose and, as a result, you will avoid triggering insulin production. You also have to be careful that insulin levels don't fall too low. This can cause other health problems.

GI scores of food tell us how quickly food is converted into glucose in the body. The low score indicates it is converted more slowly and unlikely to raise glucose levels above the insulin threshold. Eating low GI foods enables you to maintain and stabilise your energy levels throughout the day.

Imagine if you ate the following during a day:

- **Breakfast:** a commercially bought cereal and a cup of coffee
- **Lunch:** a sandwich on white bread with a packet of crisps
- **Snack:** a glass of coke/coffee and a few biscuits
- **Dinner:** a large meal of white pasta with chicken

How do you feel during the day? I can imagine after breakfast you have a lot of energy and are raring to go. Then you have a bit of a dip mid-morning; a bit of a lull. You eat at lunchtime and feel like you have picked up again. The same dip happens mid-afternoon but you feel peckish. The caffeine fills you up and suppresses the hunger a little and the biscuits give you the energy to get through until home time. Then you have a big plate of pasta (because you are starving again). You feel full and bloated afterwards. Does this sound familiar?

All of the foods/drinks mentioned above are high GI. They are causing a rise and dip in your energy levels throughout the day (the bold line on the graph). The bit you don't see is that your insulin levels are raised and fall throughout the day in line with your energy levels. Once you are in the cycle of peaks and troughs, it is difficult to break the cycle. Try not to start it off in the first place.

To avoid insulin production aim to stay away from these 5 things:

- Sugar
- Unhealthy simple carbohydrates
- Anything with caffeine
- Stress
- Smoking

I call these the **Core 5**. The Core 5 all raise your glucose levels. This will trigger insulin production and will encourage fat storage.

Chose low GI foods and drinks instead and space them evenly during the course of the day. Your energy levels and focus will remain constant throughout the day and your body will receive a constant supply of nutrients. It will also help you to feel fuller for longer since your body is receiving a steady stream of nutrients. Insulin production will be avoided all day and glucose won't be stored as fat.

### How do I maintain steady blood glucose levels?

1. **Eat protein.** It is harder for your body to break down so it is converted into glucose much slower.

2. **Eat plenty of fibre.** It slows the process of glucose extraction from your food.

3. **Eat complex carbohydrates.** These are dense in fibre so it takes longer to break them down into glucose.

Eating these 3 things every day will ensure your blood glucose levels stay fairly even and insulin production stays low, as the glucose that is released will be used as energy.

Make sure you are eating little and often and stay away from the Core 5, as mentioned above!

## GI Tables

Here is a brief overview of the carbohydrates that are low GI, medium GI and high GI, for your ease.

| Low GI Carbohydrates | |
|---|---|
| **Breads:** | Granary bread and rolls, barley bread with grains, rye bread with grains, pumpernickel bread with grains, soya bread, whole-wheat tortilla wraps |
| **Cereals:** | Bran strands, porridge |
| **Grains:** | Barley, bulgar wheat, buckwheat, quinoa |
| **Pasta and Noodles:** | Egg noodles or glass noodles |
| **Potatoes:** | New potatoes, yams |
| **Rice:** | There are no low GI rice's |
| **Sweet snacks:** | Milk, plain or white chocolate, yoghurt, low fat ice cream |
| **Savoury snacks:** | Nuts and seeds |

| Medium GI Carbohydrates | |
|---|---|
| **Breads:** | Barley, rye or pumpernickel bread (no grains), brown bread, fruit bread, pitta bread, sourdough bread, white tortilla wraps, white or brown bread with added fibre, stoneground bread |
| **Cereals:** | Bran cereal with fruit, muesli (low sugar and regular varieties), wheat cereal |
| **Grains:** | Couscous |
| **Pasta and Noodles:** | All types of pasta, soba noodles, udon noodles |
| **Potatoes:** | Crisps, sweet potatoes |
| **Rice:** | Basmati, brown, risotto, white, wild |
| **Sweet snacks:** | Biscuits, chocolate bars containing caramel or nougat, ice cream |
| **Savoury snacks:** | Potato crisps, corn chips |

| High GI Carbohydrates | |
| --- | --- |
| **Breads:** | Bagels, baguettes, gluten-free bread, white bread and rolls |
| **Cereals:** | Flaked cereals (corn, wheat or bran), honey coated cereals, puffed cereals, instant porridge |
| **Grains:** | Millet |
| **Pasta and Noodles:** | Gluten-free pasta, rice noodles |
| **Potatoes:** | Baked, French fries, mashed (real or instant) |
| **Rice:** | Fast cook varieties, jasmine rice, sticky rice |
| **Sweet snacks:** | Boiled sweets, doughnuts, jelly beans, chewy fruit sweets, waffles |
| **Savoury snacks:** | Popcorn, pretzels, rice cakes |

## Over to You

Take a look at your food intake during the week. This time look specifically at your GI levels and the Core 5. How can you reduce the amount of time you spend above the insulin threshold? What tweaks can you make to create a healthier diet?

## Summary

- Excess glucose in the bloodstream will be stored as fat.
- Eat low GI foods to maintain and stabilise blood sugar levels and to avoid insulin production.
- Eliminate the Core 5. They are triggers of insulin production.

-  Be aware of which foods are classified as low, medium and high GI.
-  Be mindful that high GI foods will raise blood sugar and insulin levels, creating the energy dips throughout the day and encouraging the storing of glucose in your fat stores.

## A Note on Sugars

Manufacturers use sugar alternatives and refined sugars in their products. They brand the products up as sugar free, reduced sugar or use other such terms. They do this to make them look more appealing to you (due to the reduced sugar quantity). Instead of sugar, the manufacturers put in alternatives to make the foods/drinks taste good. These come in the form of sugar alternatives, refined sugars and artificial sweeteners. Make sure you know all of the names below and what they are. They are not natural products and are not good for you.

Sugar alternatives and refined sugars names:

- Dextrose
- Glucose syrup
- Glucose-fructose syrup
- Inverted sugar syrup
- High fructose corn starch
- Mannitol (sugar alcohol)
- Xylitol (sugar alcohol)
- Sorbitol (sugar alcohol)
- Maltodextrin

Take a look on a food label. You will see these all mentioned directly within certain foods. A good label to see these on and to start with is a packet of sweets!

### Artificial Sweeteners
These are usually found in foods targeted towards the diet industry. Sweeteners sound much healthier than sugar somehow. Don't be fooled, they are not. Almost all of most commonly used sweeteners have been identified as having potentially harmful side effects. Here are a few of the most

common ones with a little information about them and with their associated E number.

### Aspartame (E951)

This is sold under brand names such as NutraSweet, Canderel, Equal and Spoonful. Aspartame is linked to high blood pressure, seizures, depression, numbness, aching muscles and dizziness. It is present in over 6000 food products available to the consumer.

### Sucralose (E955)

This is sold under the brand name Splenda. It is linked to shrinking the thymus gland and the enlargement of the liver and kidneys, reduced growth, decreased red blood cell count and diarrhoea.

### Acesulfame K (E950)

This is often used in soft drinks and creates reactive hypoglycaemia by stimulating insulin.

### Saccharin (E954)

This is listed as an 'anticipated human carcinogen' and can cause irritability, insomnia, headaches and itching.

### Monosodium Glutamate (MSG)

MSG is a flavour enhancer that affects appetite and may damage the hypothalamus. It has strong addictive qualities and is linked to obesity. It is only required by law to be on the ingredients list if it is in its pure form.

### How to Tell if MSG is Present in Food?

It will feature in the ingredients list as:
- Yeast extract
- Hydrolysed protein
- Whey protein isolate

- Soy protein isolate
- Carrageenan
- Most 'natural' flavourings

Be aware of these names in the ingredients list of foods. These indicate that MSG has been used within a food.

Generally on a food label, the longer the list of ingredients the more processed or preserved the product has been. Aim for foods with only a few ingredients and stay away from artificial sugars, sweeteners and refined sugars where possible.

# Protein

Most people think of protein as the nutrient that helps to build muscles. The common image that is conjured up is of Popeye and his bulging muscles. Protein does so much more than help to build muscles; it is essential in your diet. Without it your body would not function. Let us look at what proteins are, how they are formed and why it is necessary to have protein. We will also look at the different types of proteins, where they can be found and how to ensure you get the right kind in your body.

### What is Protein?

Protein is one of the 3 macronutrients. You need it in larger quantities than vitamins and minerals.

Proteins are made from molecules or building blocks called amino acids. There are 20 amino acids available from a natural diet.

Imagine you have a tub full of stickle bricks with different colours. Each colour brick is a different shape. When you fit one of each colour to a different one you create a pretty cool looking chain of different shapes. Here you have made a chain of amino acids, where each different colour is a different amino acid.

Now make another one of these chains and make sure you fit different colours together again. Once you have done this combine the 2 chains together. You have just made a protein! The formation of proteins occur when many chains of amino acids combine, just like the stickle bricks.

There are many functions of protein in the body. The shape or structure of a protein will dictate its function within the body. When you put the stickle bricks together in different patterns and shapes, you are creating different proteins that will have very different functions within the body.

## Why Do We Need Protein?

Protein has many functions within the body. Without it the body can't function. Here are a few of protein's main functions:

- Forming the structural framework of tissue, forming cells, maintaining tissues and repairing damage to tissues.
- Enabling your muscle fibres to shorten in order to create movement and help you to move your muscles.
- Transporting substances through your blood; such as oxygen, carbon dioxide, sodium and potassium.
- Regulating your hormones for physiological processes. Hormones help to coordinate certain bodily activities; for example, insulin is produced to control the blood-sugar concentration in the body.
- Assisting your body in protecting itself from infection; antibodies are specialised proteins.
- Formation of enzymes (biological catalysts) that speed up chemical reactions in your body. These help to digest your food and allow compounds to combine with another.

## Other Benefits

If you have ever 'dieted' in your life, you may be aware of the importance of protein in your diet. It is renowned to help you to manage hunger. Protein will keep you fuller for longer since it takes a lot of effort and time to break down. Protein also helps to maintain muscle mass, which is known to increase metabolism. Protein provides the body with energy; for every one gram of protein, it contains 4 calories.

# Get ready for the science bit!

### Formation of Proteins

How does the body form protein from the food that we eat?

When you eat something, your body breaks down the dietary protein into the separate amino acids, which are absorbed into the blood and enter the cells. The nucleus in the cell sends out information, telling the cell which type of protein to build. Animal and plant cells join these amino acids together to form peptides. This process results in the formation of chains of amino acids of varying lengths, which eventually become proteins. The number and sequence of the amino acids will make one protein different from another.

| How Peptides Combine | | |
|---|---|---|
| **Peptides** | **Name** | **Meaning** |
| Two amino acids | Dipeptide | Di meaning two |
| Three amino acids | Tripeptide | Tri meaning three |
| 4 - 9 amino acids | Oligopeptide | Oligo meaning few |
| 10 or more amino acids | Polypeptide | Poly meaning many |

Proteins are formed when the chain of amino acids total 100 or more, or when two polypeptide chains combine and repeatedly fold together to form specific 3D shapes. The shape that is created determines the function of the protein.

### Classifications of Protein

9 of the amino acids are known as 'essential amino acids'. Your body can't make these. You need to get these from your diet so that your body can make the other 11 'non-essential amino acids'. As long as you successfully absorb sufficient

amounts of the 9 essential amino acids, your liver is able to synthesise the remaining 11 non-essential amino acids.

## Complete and Incomplete Proteins

### Complete Proteins

These contain all of the 9 essential amino acids in sufficient amounts necessary for your liver to make the remaining non-essential amino acids. Most of these are animal based foods, although there are a few plant based complete proteins.

Where you can find complete proteins:
- Meat
- Poultry
- Fish
- Dairy
- Eggs
- Soy Foods
- Buckwheat
- Quinoa

### Incomplete Proteins

Plants contain many nutrients, including protein. These proteins are of a lower biological value, since they are deficient or 'incomplete' in one or more of the essential amino acids that the body needs. Therefore, incomplete proteins are plant-based proteins and don't contain all the essential amino acids. They have a smaller concentration of protein. This makes it difficult to ingest enough from plant produce alone.

Where you can find incomplete proteins:
- Cereals and grains (wheat, rye, barley, oats, rice)
- Cereal products (bread, pasta)
- Pulses (beans, lentils, peas)

- Nuts and seeds
- Vegetables

**Complementary Proteins**
Incomplete proteins (the plant based proteins) can be combined to provide the full spectrum of essential amino acids necessary for a healthy diet. This is advisable if you are a vegetarian and doing so will boost your amino acid intake.

Whilst these carbohydrate-based foods contain energy in the form of glucose, they also contain smaller amounts of protein. If you are on a low meat or no meat diet make sure you include a variety of unrefined carbohydrate foods in your diet.

**Good Combinations**
- Rice and pulses
- Vegetables and seeds
- Nuts and vegetables
- Grains and pulses

## Over to You

Take a look at the food you eat during a week. This time look specifically at your protein intake. What sources of protein are you consuming? Are you getting all the amino acids your body needs? What tweaks can you make to ensure you do?

## Summary

How can you use all of this knowledge?

💜 Most people get the majority of their protein from their evening meal. This alone is not enough protein. Aim to get protein into every meal and snack throughout the day.

❤ Aim to get your daily intake from a variety of sources. Try to eat half animal-based and half plant-based sources.

❤ Know what combinations of proteins will give you the full spectrum of amino acids that are needed.

❤ Eat 'clean' animal proteins: fish and poultry

❤ Stay away from processed meats or ones high in saturated fat (red meats generally): bacon, beef, duck, game, ham, lamb, mince and pork.

❤ If you are a vegetarian, make sure you know how to combine proteins to give you all the amino acids your body needs every day.

❤ Aim for your daily diet to comprise of around 20% protein. Try to get the same amount of protein in your diet as essential fats.

# Fats

### Why Such Bad Press?
Fats get a hard time generally and have had a bad press in recent history. When people 'diet' they commonly think they need to cut out the fat in their diet to lose any excess fat they have. This is not the case. We are going to look at fats and why they are so important in any eating routine. We will look at the different types of fats, which ones are good for you and which ones you should limit.

### What are Fats and Lipids?
Fats/lipids are one of the macronutrients, just like carbohydrates and proteins. Lipid is a collective name for fats and oils. Fats are solid at room temperature and oils are fluid at room temperature. Lipids are a dense source of energy; for every 1 gram of fat it provides 9 calories. They provide more calories than protein and carbohydrates (both on 4 calories).

### Why Do We Need Fats?
Fats are very important for your body. They do so much more than people are aware of.

Here are the main ones to know about.
- Nervous system: fats make up the majority of your Central Nervous System and spinal cord.
- Cells: fats are an integral component of virtually all cell membranes.
- Vitamins: fat transports, absorbs and helps to utilise vitamins A, D, E and K (the fat soluble vitamins).
- Protect your internal organs.
- Insulate through your subcutaneous adipose tissue.
- Fuel source during lower intensity workloads.
- Store energy within the adipose tissue.

- Form the myelin sheath within the nervous system, which allows impulses to transmit quickly and efficiently along the nerve cells.
- Aid the synthesis of steroid hormones – essential for proper body functioning.
- Assist in the regulation of enzymes.

Fats play a massive part in the body. If you choose not to eat them, you are choosing for all the above to be starved of an essential nutrient that you need for your body to function. The key therefore is not to CUT out fat but to choose the right ones!

## Are you ready for the science bit?

### Structure of Fats
The smaller units of fats are called fatty acids. Their molecule lengths differ and there exists double strength bonds between some atoms. These double bonds change the shape of the molecule. A different shape means a different function in the body. This last bit is very important when we start to look at the types of fat.

### Types of Fat
There are 3 major categories of fat:
- Saturated Fats
- Unsaturated Fats
- Trans Fats

### Saturated Fat
This is where a chain of carbon molecules is fully saturated with hydrogen atoms. This causes the chains to be straight; there are no double bonds in a saturated fat. Imagine that saturated fat is like a long, straight piece of string. Since all the molecules are in a straight line, they can pack closely together. This means they are solid at room temperature.

Saturated fats are the ones that tend to get the bad press. They are seen as evil and we are told we should avoid them. You do need a certain amount of saturated fat in your diet for your body to function well. It is when you eat it in large quantities that it starts to cause issues and health complications, such as heart disease.

Your fat intake spilt should be 25% saturated fat and 75% unsaturated fats.

### Sources of Saturated Fat

Animal products are well known for their saturated fat content. The following all contain saturated fat.

- Meat: beef, pork, lamb, venison
- Poultry: chicken, turkey, duck
- Dairy: milk, cheese, yoghurt, cream, butter
- Eggs

Saturated fat is also present in non-animal products, such as palm oil and coconut oil.

### Unsaturated Fat

Some hydrogen atoms are absent from the chain of carbons detailed above. Where this occurs a double bond is formed between one or more of the carbon atoms. This creates a bend in the chain at each double bond. Wherever there is a missing hydrogen atom, there will be a bend. This can occur once or many times in a chain.

You will have heard the terms monounsaturated and polyunsaturated when you hear about fats. Monounsaturated simply means there is one single double bond (and therefore only one bend in the chain) and polyunsaturated means there are several double bonds in the chain (and therefore several bends in the chain). This means that they are both liquid at room temperature; they can't pack tightly together like the saturated fats do.

Sources of monounsaturated fatty acids
- Olives and olive oil
- Peanut oil
- Rapeseed oil
- Avocados
- Nuts
- Seeds

They are less stable than saturated fats and care is needed to store them properly. Make sure you store oils in cool conditions and away from direct sunlight. Heat, light and oxygen can create oxidative damage to them.

### Polyunsaturated Fatty Acids
There are 2 subdivisions of these that you will have heard about:

- Essential fatty acids (EFA)
- Non-essential fatty acids

### Essential Fatty Acids
These are essential since your body can't synthesise them. You must consume them in your diet. These are specific to the functioning of the cell and must be eaten in the required amounts to promote good health. They are subdivided into 2 categories:

- **Omega 3 fatty acids:** these support your heart, brain and eyes

- **Omega 6 fatty acids:** these are good for your hair and skin

They are also known to help with a whole raft of ailments and studies have shown they have had a positive impact on health issues, such as asthma, diabetes, arthritis, osteoporosis, some cancers and high cholesterol.

### Sources of Omega 3 Fatty Acids
- Seafood, especially oily fish: halibut, herring, mackerel, oysters, salmon, sardines, trout, fresh tuna
- Flaxseed oil
- Rapeseed oil
- Nuts: walnuts especially
- Pasture reared eggs

### Sources of Omega 6 Fatty Acids
- Olives and olive oil
- Sunflower seeds and sunflower oil
- Pumpkin seeds
- Safflower oil
- Sesame seeds and sesame oil
- Flaxseed
- Avocado
- Nuts
- Chicken
- Eggs

All oils need to be cold pressed and remain unprocessed for them to be of good quality.

### Non-Essential Fatty Acids
Your body needs these to function but you can produce them directly from the foods you eat – provided you eat well! They are known as Omega 5, Omega 7 and Omega 9 fatty acids.

**Omega 5** is known to have a positive effect on weight related cardiovascular health and blood sugar balance.

**Omega 7** has a positive effect on healthy weight loss and bowel regularity. It also has anti-ageing properties and therefore plays a role in nourishing healthy cells, especially in the digestive tract.

**Omega 9** is linked to healthy cardiovascular systems, healthy cholesterol levels, improved immune function and healthy blood sugar levels.

### Sources of Non-Essential Fatty Acids
- **Omega 5:** full fat grass-fed dairy, wild salmon, macadamia nuts, pomegranate seeds/oil.
- **Omega 7:** grass-fed meat, full fat grass-fed dairy, wild caught salmon, macadamia nuts.
- **Omega 9:** olives, olive oil, avocado, grass-fed meat, nuts, sesame oil.

As you can see there is a crossover with the sources and the type of Omega fatty acid they will provide. If you aim to eat some of the foods off the lists above, you will be getting at least one (if not more without you knowing!) of the Omegas into your diet.

### Trans Fat
There is one other fat that MUST be talked about and that is 'Trans Fat'.

These are the ones that have given fats a bad name and food manufacturers are diluting the food pool with so many of these. They should be avoided like the plague. Don't go near them. If offered them, politely decline. They are BAD for your health.

### How Trans Fats are Made
Imagine you have a bottle of olive oil. It is liquid at room temperature, right? Food manufacturers take oils, like olive

oil, and put them through a process called 'hydrogenation.' This is where they heat the oil to a very high temperature in large vats. The heat pushes the molecules in the oil further apart making them highly reactive. At this point, a nickel catalyst is added to the vat to increase the reaction speed.

Hydrogen gas is then pumped through the oil. The hydrogen attaches to the carbon fat chains at the point of the weak double bonds (remember the oils have double bonds which means they have bends in the chains). The bent carbon chain becomes fully saturated with these hydrogen atoms. The resulting fatty acid is a straight one; it resembles a saturated fat and is solid at room temperature. So what started as a mono or polyunsaturated oil ends up with a straight chain just like a saturated fat.

You will have seen this on the shelves in shops as margarine, amongst many other products. With margarine the oils are partially hydrogenated so some fatty acids remain unsaturated. This makes the product not quite a solid, but definitely not an oil. The manufacturers have messed with its chemical make-up. This allows companies to still market it as a polyunsaturated spread, unfortunately.

Now, remember when I said that the shape of the fat chain determines the function in the body? During hydrogenation the unsaturated double bonds that the oil started with have become altered. The resulting shape is a straight chain. The altered shape fools the body and it can no longer perform the correct chemical reaction that it associates with an unsaturated chain. So it sits in your body, being unused because your body doesn't know what to do with it.

## Health Concerns
Trans fats are not good for you. They are linked to coronary heart disease, the hardening of your arteries, cancer, atherosclerosis, diabetes, obesity and immune system

dysfunction. There are many other illnesses and diseases trans fats are linked to. None of which you would choose to have!

**Where You Will Find Trans Fats**
- Many margarines
- Biscuits, cakes, crackers
- Take away foods
- Boxed meals and TV dinners
- Ice creams
- Pies, pastries
- Pre-prepared foods
- Many low fat processed foods
- Sweet sauces and syrups
- Some ready-made sauces

Be aware of where they are and stay well clear!

## Over to You

Take a look at the food you eat during a week. This time look specifically at your fat intake. What sources of fat are you consuming? Do you tend to eat one kind more than the others? What tweaks can you make to ensure you are eating a healthy balance between them? Which trans fats can you eliminate from your diet straight away?

## Summary

- You need fat in your diet for optimum health. Don't cut it out.
- Trans fats and hydrogenated products – STAY AWAY! Do not eat any of these.
- Split the fats into 25% saturated fat and 75% unsaturated fat in your diet.
- Aim for around 30 - 35% fat in your daily diet.
- Experiment with new foods and have fun with it!

## Vitamins and Minerals

Vitamins and minerals are known as the micronutrients. This means you don't need to eat as many of them as the three macronutrients. They are, however, equally essential to good health.

Vitamins and minerals are present in the foods you eat every day. Some foods have more vitamins and minerals in than others.

### What are Vitamins?
Vitamins are organic substances (made by plants or animals) and can be obtained in the diet either by eating the plant itself or eating animal products that have gained their vitamin content from plants.

Vitamins have many benefits to health. They boost the immune system, support growth and repair, extract energy from the macronutrients, help with metabolism and protect against free radicals, to name a few.

Vitamins fall into two categories. Those that are fat-soluble and those that are water-soluble. The fat-soluble vitamins (A, D, E and K) dissolve in fat and can be stored in the body. They can only be transported, absorbed and utilised in the presence of fat. A diet low in fat will result in severe deficiency in the fat-soluble vitamins, which will lead to ill health.

Fat-soluble vitamins are mainly found in fatty foods, such as animal fats (including butter, vegetable oils, dairy foods, liver and oily fish). Your body needs these vitamins every day to work at 100%. However, you do not need to eat foods containing them every day; your body is capable of storing them up for future use.

The water-soluble vitamins – B complex (made up of a number of types, including B6, B12, riboflavin, folic acid etc.) and C vitamins are transported, absorbed and utilised within water. They are all absorbed along the length of the digestive tract and tend to have an effect within the cells themselves. They can't be stored in the body in great quantities so we need to include them in our daily diet. Any vitamin B or C that your body doesn't use as it passes through your system is lost so you need a fresh supply of these vitamins every day.

Water-soluble vitamins are found in fruit, vegetables and grains. Unlike the fat-soluble vitamins, water-soluble vitamins can be destroyed by heat and by being exposed to the air and they can be lost in the water used for cooking. When you cook foods, especially by boiling them, you will lose many of the vitamins. Instead, steam or grill the foods to keep as many of the vitamins as intact as possible.

**What are Minerals?**
Minerals are inorganic substances that come from the soil and water and are absorbed by plants or eaten by animals.

Minerals are needed for three main reasons. They build strong bones and teeth. They control the body fluids inside and outside cells. They do not provide us with energy but do allow us to unlock the energy contained within the diet.

Your body needs larger amounts of some minerals than others. The essential minerals are calcium, sulphur, sodium, potassium, phosphorous, chloride and magnesium. Minerals are found in different quantities in foods such as meat, cereals (including cereal products such as bread), fish, milk, dairy foods, vegetables, fruit and nuts.

There are other minerals your body needs but in smaller quantities. These are the trace minerals. Trace minerals include copper, manganese, iron, selenium, zinc, iodine, cobalt and fluoride. These can be found in smaller amounts in meat, fish, cereals, milk, dairy foods, vegetables and nuts.

You should be able to get all the vitamins and minerals your body needs by eating a varied and balanced diet every day. This is the key!

A word about recommended daily allowances. These are viewed as a general guideline as to the nutrient levels needed to offset deficiency and disease. They don't take into account exercise or your frame. The guidelines do not suggest what is needed to maintain optimum health.

Many people take vitamin and mineral supplements. The key to taking supplements is to remember they are there to supplement the diet and NOT replace it. Supplementation is a very complex area and you should speak to your GP or nutritionist if you want to explore supplementation in more detail.

## Over to You

Take a look at the food you eat during a week. Are you getting a good range of vitamins and minerals into your body? What tweaks can you make to ensure you do?

## Summary

- You need to make sure you have a variety of fresh foods in your diet every day.
- This will provide all the vitamins and minerals your body needs to stay healthy.
- Supplements are not there to replace elements in your diet. Use them as an addition to your diet.

# Drinks

There are many different drinks available in the shops these days. There are still drinks, fizzy drinks, ones that promise to give you energy, ones that make you wobble if you drink too many of them, ones that are colourful and vibrant looking and ones that look like sludge. How do you know which ones are good and which ones are not so good for your body and mind? We will start off by looking at what is good to drink and progress from there!

**Water.** It is all around us in many different forms and guises. Water is neither a macro nor micronutrient. It is, however, essential for life. You can probably go without food for a few weeks and survive. The average human body can probably go one week without water and then it will shut down. It is vital to life. Water makes up a large proportion of your body weight: 60 - 70%. The human brain is about 85% water and your bones are about 10 - 15% water. Women usually have a lower percentage of water in their body since they have more adipose tissue than men.

Water is the medium through which all other nutrients, chemicals and oxygen are transported around your body. Your body needs an adequate daily intake for optimum health and wellbeing.

Water has so many benefits. Here are a few. It suppresses appetite. It reduces the build-up of sodium in your body. It helps to maintain muscle tone. It helps to eliminate waste and toxins. It relieves fluid retention. It balances body temperature. It assists in digestion and absorption of food. It lubricates your joints and muscles. It moves the water-soluble vitamins, nutrients, hormones, chemicals and oxygen around your body. It makes up the majority of your brain. It is fundamental for cell and body health. Do you see how important it is?

So how can you ensure you get enough water in to your body every day? Aim to drink a minimum of one and a half litres per day. This will keep you lubricated, help with hunger and keep you active (you will need to visit the toilet!) If you exercise or it is hot and humid, you will need to drink more to replenish what you lose through sweating. You may become dehydrated before you become thirsty. If you reach the thirsty stage, you are already dehydrated.

Keep drinking throughout the day. Keep a water bottle on you when you are moving around during the day and a glass of water on your desk or near you at home. You are more likely to drink it if it is there.

If you don't like the taste of clear water, try adding a slice of lemon, orange or lime to it. Be careful of adding lots of cordial to it. They tend to have sugar in them. Also try adding a tiny splash of fruit juice into your water. It will make it taste different but will still ensure you are getting the water intake you need. Be careful of adding too much fruit juice; your body will take the sugar from it and could store it for use later. If you don't use it straight away, it will store it away in the fat stores.

**Tea and coffee** don't count towards the recommended water intake, as they are diuretics that encourage the passing of water out of the body. For every cup of tea or coffee you have, make sure you drink a glass of water afterwards to rehydrate your body. If you don't do this, it will lead to dehydration.

**Alcohol** doesn't count towards water intake either. For every gram of alcohol you drink you are having 7 calories. Limit your alcohol intake as much as possible.

If you don't drink enough water, your body will go into the starvation response, just as it does with food, by holding onto the water you drink. You will experience this as bloating and water retention. When you are giving your body enough fluid on a regular basis, your body lets go of any it is holding onto because it knows there is a steady supply of it coming in. The minute you start to restrict access to it, your body will hold onto everything it has. This is the same process your body goes through with food (remember the starvation response?)

Water is hugely important – I can't stress enough that you should reach for this above everything else.

## Frequently Asked Questions

### *Can I drink fruit juice?*

Yes, but just be aware of the following. Fruit juice from concentrate is high in sugar. Go for fruit juices not from concentrate. Limit your consumption of fruit juice because of the sugar content. Good quality fruit juice counts towards your 5 a day fruit and vegetable intake.

### *Are diet fizzy drinks better for me than full fat varieties?*

No. All fizzy drinks (including diet) typically contain water, sugar/sweetener, flavouring agent, caffeine, colourings, preservatives and other ingredients that are not good for you. The health effects of fizzy drinks are well recorded. The common health issues related to drinking fizzy drinks are obesity and weight related diseases, bone loss and tooth decay. Multiple artificial sweeteners are used in diet drinks instead of the sugar. This will still give the sweet taste that you expect from a fizzy drink. Aspartame, Saccharin, Sucralose and Acesulfame K are the most commonly used artificial sweeteners. These have been suggested to be carcinogens and have many health issues associated with them. Fizzy drinks contain trans fats so you can expect extra health issues relating to these too. Stay away from fizzy drinks at all costs. They are not natural products and have many health related issues associated with them.

### Are decaffeinated drinks better for me than caffeine drinks?

Decaffeinated drinks have been subjected to processing to strip away the caffeine. There is usually some caffeine still present in decaffeinated drinks. It is very hard to strip all of it away. Since decaffeination is achieved by processing, it has been subjected to abnormal processes (i.e. not natural). There are arguments to say that caffeine is good for certain aspects of health and other arguments that say decaffeinated is better. I suggest you know the side effects of caffeine and decide for yourself whether you drink it.

Caffeine is a stimulant that affects the central nervous system. Caffeine can be found in coffee, tea, fizzy drinks, painkillers, energy tablets and drinks and chocolate, to name a few.

Having lots of caffeine on a regular basis can have the same effect on your body as stress can. It elevates your heart rate, can make you feel nervous, irritable, agitated, shaky, give you headaches, make your muscles twitch, flush your face, upset your stomach, speed up your breathing and influence your sleep. Your body gets used to caffeine and if you cut it out instantly you can get withdrawal effects. This could be experienced as a throbbing headache, tiredness or drowsiness, anxiety, depression or feeling sick. These feelings can last up to a week. If you think caffeine affects you, you should wean yourself off it slowly. Caffeine dependence can be avoided by limiting the amount of caffeine you have daily, or by taking periodic breaks from caffeinated drinks.

If you do decide to drink caffeine or decaffeinated, drink the fresh varieties and not instant and always ensure you drink water to rehydrate afterwards. If you want to find an alternative hot drink, why not try naturally caffeine free alternatives such as chamomile tea (well known for its relaxing properties) or green tea (well known for its antioxidant and weight loss properties)?

### Is skimmed cow's milk better than full fat cow's milk?

The different milks vary according to the way they are produced and their fat content. Cow's milk is higher in calcium than most other kinds of milk and is rich in protein.

In the UK, natural whole milk has a minimum fat content of 3.5%, semi-skimmed milk has a fat content of about 1.7% and skimmed milk has a fat content between 0 - 0.5%. There is also a 1% fat milk on the market, which can't be described as whole, semi-skimmed or skimmed milk.

Full fat milk is high in saturated fat. For older children and adults, having too much saturated fat can contribute to becoming overweight. It can also cause raised levels of cholesterol in the blood, which can put you at increased risk of a heart attack and a stroke.

If you are trying to cut down on fat, go for the lower fat milks, such as semi-skimmed, 1% fat and skimmed milks, which contain all the important nutritional benefits of milk but are lower in fat.

There are other types of milk on the market: goat's milk, soy milk, oat milk, rice milk and almond milk. These have different nutritional properties and offer an alternative if you are lactose intolerant.

### Can I drink alcohol?
Yes. Be aware of how much you are drinking though and ensure you are not trying to mask underlying issues and problems with it. Drink in moderation and sensibly. Be aware

that alcohol contains calories that the body won't use, so you may put weight on and have health issues associated with this. You can eat and drink anything you like, provided you have a balanced and varied diet.

The 80-20 rule is a good one to think about here. If you cut out alcohol completely, you may crave it and end up binging on it. The 80-20 rule is very simple and is something that you can apply to all aspects of your life. 80% of the time aim to eat/drink healthily and the remaining 20% of the time you can eat/drink what you like. If alcohol is your treat of choice, make sure you stick to the 80-20 rule throughout the rest of the week and drink lots of water to rehydrate and flush the alcohol through your system.

## Over to You

Take a look at the fluids you put into your body during a week. What patterns do you see? What could you do to make sure you are drinking plenty of water? What tweaks can you make?

## Summary

- ♥ Drink water every day. It is essential to life and optimum health.
- ♥ The starvation response will kick in if you don't drink enough water.
- ♥ Drink a glass of water after tea or coffee to ensure you hydrate yourself.
- ♥ Stay away from fizzy drinks. These contain many nasties.
- ♥ Drink alcohol in moderation and sensibly. Don't use it to mask issues in your life.
- ♥ Balance and variety is the key to living a healthy life. Don't cut out foods or drinks. You will crave them.
- ♥ Live by the 80-20 rule.

# Chapter 7: Balancing the Diet

It is well known that people in the Western World eat more than they should.

The reason? Many don't know what constitutes a portion and how this looks on a plate.

Most people tend to fill their plate when serving food, regardless of how big the plate is. Once the plate is full, it is so easy to sit and try to eat everything on it because you have been brought up to 'clean your plate'. If you serve on 'big' plates, this could be the start of many issues.

So how can you be sure you are eating the right amount of each food group in your diet? This is the area that causes the most concern and most people struggle with.

We will look at a few general tips to help you with this and a few resources that you should be aware of that will give you guidance.

First, let's look at what we need in the diet and in what quantities.

We need to eat food from 5 different groups. These are:

1. Fruit and vegetables.
2. Starchy foods, such as rice, pasta, bread and potatoes.
3. Meat, fish, eggs and beans.
4. Milk and dairy foods.
5. Foods containing sugar and fat.

Most people in the UK eat and drink too many calories and have too much fat, sugar and salt in the diet. They are generally lacking in fruit, vegetables and fibre.

**The National Guidelines**

The Eat Well Plate was designed by the Food Standards Agency (FSA). The Eat Well Plate is a visual guide that shows the different types of food you need to eat and in what proportions. These are guidelines to achieve a balanced and healthy diet.

You should be aiming to eat at least 5 portions of a variety of fruit and vegetables every day. Fruit and vegetables should make up one third of everything you eat. Starchy foods should make up around one third of everything you eat. This means you should base your meals on these foods. Choose whole grain varieties as much as you can.

The other third of your diet should be made up of the following. Meat, fish, eggs and beans should make up around 12% of the foods you eat. Aim for at least 2 portions of fish a week, including 1 portion of oily fish. Milk and dairy foods should make up around 15% of the foods you eat. Fat and sugar should make up around 8% of the foods you eat.

## The Eat Well Plate - Visual Guide

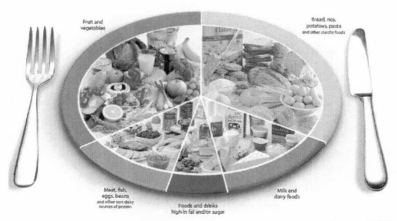

**Source: NHS**

**Portion Size**
It would be useful for you to know what a portion looks like.

Here is a detailed table so you can see what a portion would look like.

| Detailed Guide - What ONE Portion Looks Like | |
| --- | --- |
| Fruit | **Small fruit:** 2 satsumas, 2 plums, 2 kiwi fruits, 7 strawberries, 14 cherries<br>**Medium fruit:** 1 apple, 1 banana, 1 pear, 1 orange<br>**Large fruit:** half a grapefruit, one 5cm slice of melon, 1 large slice of pineapple<br>**Dried fruit:** about 30g, one large heaped tablespoon of raisins or sultanas, handful of banana chips<br>**Fruit juice:** 150 ml of unsweetened juice |
| Vegetables | **Green veg:** 2 broccoli spears, 4 heaped tablespoons of kale, spinach or green beans<br>**Salad veg:** 3 sticks of celery, 5cm piece of cucumber, 1 medium tomato, 7 cherry tomatoes<br>**Cooked veg:** 3 heaped tablespoons carrots, peas, corn or cauliflower |
| Bread, rice, pasta and potatoes | 1 slice of bread<br>Handful of rice or pasta<br>Handful of breakfast cereal<br>1 small to medium potato |
| Meat, fish, eggs and beans | Lean meat the size of a deck of cards<br>1 large egg<br>Side of fish the size of a standard chequebook<br>Handful of beans, nuts or seeds |
| Milk and dairy | Small cup of milk<br>150ml of yoghurt<br>Piece of cheese the size of small matchbox |
| Food and drinks high in fat or sugar | Limit these to no more than 8% of total intake |

As you look at this, think about the food and portions that you eat.

Do you tend to have 1 slice of bread for a portion?
Do you have a handful of nuts and seeds? Or two?
Do you have 150ml of fruit juice?

The detailed portion guide above helps to acknowledge the difference between how much you are eating and how much you should be eating. Become familiar with it!

### Easy Guide to Portion Sizes
Here are some quick ideas that will help you when you are out and about to gauge portion size.

**Fruit:** your fist is about the same size as a portion of fruit.
**Cheese:** your thumb (from the base to the tip) is the size of a portion of cheese.
**Meat, fish or poultry:** your palm (minus all the fingers) is the size of a portion.
**Nuts:** your cupped hand is the size of a portion.

### Use Your Hands!
I like to use my hands to see how big meals should be. Here is a rough idea of how big meals should be using your hands.

- Breakfast should be the area of around 80% of both cupped hands together
- Lunch should be the area of 100% of both hands spread flat
- Dinner should be the area of 100% of both hands spread flat
- Snacks should be the area of around 80% of 1 cupped hand. Aim for less than 200 calories per snack.

**What This Looks Like on a Plate**

On your plate, this is what you want to see for each of the meals/snacks that you eat.

- For **breakfast** you should aim for 30% complex starchy carbohydrates, 30% complex carbohydrates and 40% protein.
- For **lunch** you should aim for 40% protein, 40% complex carbohydrates and 20% starchy complex carbohydrates.
- For **dinner** you should aim for 60% complex carbohydrates and 40% protein.
- For **snacks** you should aim for 60% complex carbohydrates and 40% protein.

**General Ideas for Portion Size**

Ensure you eat every 3-4 hours and try to incorporate 3 meals and 2 snacks in to every day (breakfast, mid-morning snack, lunch, mid-afternoon snack and dinner). This will keep your hunger under control, make you less hungry at meal times and encourage smaller portions. Hunger will be reduced due to sustained blood sugar levels and your metabolism will be better maintained.

Buy smaller plates and dish up smaller portions. If you dish up on big plates you are guaranteed to serve more. You are also more likely to try to eat it all and not stop when you are full.

Serve meals already dished up on the plate so you can see how much you have. If you eat buffet style or serve in little dishes for people to help themselves, portions are much less likely to be monitored. That is because it is so much easier to reach for more than you would normally eat when meals are serviced like this, than it is if all the food is already on the plate at the start.

Eat the healthy foods and the ones low in calories on the plate first. Then if you are full before the end, you will have eaten the most nutritious parts.

If you are eating out and you are full but have food left on the plate/in the dishes, request to take home the bits you have left. Don't feel the need to eat it all. There is the thought that 'I have paid for it so I must eat it'. If you are full, your body won't thank you for squishing in the extra few mouthfuls. Instead, request to take it home and have it the next day.

Don't forget the points I mentioned in earlier sections about how to eat too. These will help you to slow down and eat less.

As a reminder here are the key points.
- Eat slowly and savour every bite.
- While you eat, focus on your meal.
- Stop eating as soon as you become full. You are more likely to know when this is if you eat slower.
- When you finish eating and want to reach for something else, wait 10-20 minutes and then decide if you are still hungry. This will enable your mind to catch up with your belly.
- Live by the 80-20 rule.

## Over to You

Take a look at your portion sizes. Are you eating within the recommended guidelines? If not, what tweaks can you make to ensure you do?

## Summary

- Watching your portion sizes is fundamental to living a healthy lifestyle.
- Become familiar with the national guidelines and the Eat Well Plate.
- Be conscious of how much you are eating and measure out portions until it becomes familiar to you.
- Be aware of the proportions of each nutrient you need in each meal and snack until it becomes ingrained.
- Know how to measure a portion easily.
- Buy smaller plates.
- Dish up food straight onto plates.
- Eat the healthier foods on the plate first.
- Take home extra food when eating out.

# Chapter 8: Meal Ideas

People frequently ask me what they should be eating that would form a healthy and nutritious meal. Here are a few ideas of things you could eat for each meal and snacks that are healthy and nutritionally balanced.

These are taken from the kinds of foods I enjoy. Don't forget that everyone is different and will have different tastes. Find foods that you like and experiment with the cooking and combinations of foods that work for you.

Below I have outlined the meal types, the key ingredients for that meal, the proportions recommended and a few ideas of combinations you could try.

# Breakfast

**Key Ingredients:**
**Complex starchy carbohydrates:** oat flakes, barley flakes, bran flakes, buckwheat flakes, sugar free cereal, millet, rye flakes, rye bread, whole grain bread, porridge, muesli.
**Complex carbohydrates:** fruit.
**Protein:** nuts, seeds, eggs, fish, lean meat, yoghurt, milk.

**Proportions:**
For breakfast you should aim for 30% complex starchy carbohydrates, 30% complex carbohydrates and 40% protein.

**Ideas:**
- Yoghurt – 2-3 tablespoons of live low fat natural yoghurt with a handful of fruit, a tablespoon of nuts and seeds.
- Porridge oats with milk, berries, nuts and seeds.
- Wholemeal toast with nut butter (2 slices).

- Fruit smoothie – 2 handfuls of fruit and a couple of tablespoons of live low fat natural yoghurt, tablespoon of seeds and milk.
- Unsweetened cereal (about 4 tablespoons) with handful of nuts and milk.
- 2 eggs (poached, scrambled or soft boiled) with toast or crackers.

# Lunch

Key Ingredients:
**Protein:** chicken, fish, pulses, tofu, Quinoa, shellfish, cheese.
**Complex carbohydrates:** vegetables, salad.
**Starchy complex carbohydrates:** whole-wheat pasta, whole grain bread, brown rice, potatoes, pitta pockets, rye bread, pumpernickel bread, whole grain tortilla, sweet potatoes, beans, lentils.

**Proportions:**
For lunch you should aim for 40% protein, 40% complex carbohydrates and 20% starchy complex carbohydrates.

**Ideas:**
- Home prepared salad with nuts, seeds, meat/fish, beans, olive oil, avocado with brown rice.
- Whole-wheat sandwich with protein and salad (minus dressings or margarine/butter). Use seasoning (mustard etc.) instead.
- Small jacket potato with protein and salad.
- Whole-wheat pasta with cooked vegetables and a light sauce, such as olive oil. Don't use pre-bought sauces.
- Vegetable based soup with fresh whole-wheat chunk of bread.

## Dinner

**Key Ingredients:**
**Complex carbohydrates:** vegetables, salad.
**Protein:** lean meat, fish, eggs, pulses, tofu, shellfish, cheese.

**Proportions:**
For dinner you should aim for 60% complex carbohydrates and 40% protein.

**Ideas:**
- Stir fry – some protein with vegetables (no noodles for dinner).
- Grilled chicken breast with salad or vegetables.
- Red or grey mullet, sardines, swordfish (grilled or baked) with large portion of grilled vegetables over a mixed leaf salad.
- Pulse (beans, chickpeas etc) casserole with vegetables.

## Snacks

**Key Ingredients:**
**Complex carbohydrates:** fruit, vegetables, oatcakes, rye crackers.
**Protein:** nuts, seeds, eggs, fish, lean meat, pulses, cottage cheese, yoghurt.

**Proportions:**
For snacks you should aim for 60% complex carbohydrates and 40% protein.

**Ideas:**
- Crackers with nut butter, cottage cheese, chicken or fish.
- Yoghurt, fruit and seeds – small pot of live natural low fat yoghurt, handful of berries and a sprinkle of seeds over top.

- Piece of fruit (banana, apple, pear etc.) with handful of nuts.
- Nuts and seed mix – high calorie content so limit these.
- Houmous (tablespoon) with a handful of raw chopped vegetable crudités.
- Fruit shakes – homemade with either yoghurt or milk.

The key thing to remember is not to eat starchy complex carbohydrates for your evening meal. Eat them at lunchtime instead. You could interchange the meals I have suggested for lunch and dinner by serving them with or without starchy complex carbohydrates depending on which meal you are eating it for.

## Over to You

So there are some ideas of the kind of things I eat for meals and snacks. Take a look at this and come up with some new ideas (for meals and snacks) that are healthy and balanced that you can introduce straight away into your diet.

# Eating Out

Many restaurants, cafes and pub menus don't reflect a healthy and balanced meal. Frequently, I go into places to eat and find that, while the ingredients they source and use are fresh and local and the food is made on the premises, the meals they have put together are usually lacking in nutrients and they don't choose the healthiest ingredients.

Let me demonstrate. Think about the vegetarian options you have noted recently in restaurants. They tend to consist of carbohydrates (so maybe pasta or risotto) but don't tend to have any protein in them. This could be easily achieved by adding nuts and seeds or beans and pulses to the dish.

When you are looking for something healthy and nutritious on the menu ask yourself and the waiter/waitress the following questions:

- Is it brown or white (pasta, bread, rice etc)?
- Does it contain homemade sauces and dressings or are they out of a jar?
- Does it contain protein, carbohydrates and healthy fats?
- How large is the meal portion?
- Is it freshly prepared on the premises?
- Are the ingredients of the best quality? For example, is it home cooked ham instead of processed, sliced ham?
- Can the sauce or dressing be served separately, so you can add it to your taste? For example, salad dressings.

Armed with the answers to these questions, you will be able to make a more informed decision.

Opt for dishes that are grilled, baked, steamed, poached , roasted , boiled, have a wine based sauce or are stir fried.

Avoid dishes that are fried, sautéed, batter dipped, creamed, cheesed, marinated in oil, have a 'special' sauce, are crispy or cream based dishes.

## Frequently Asked Questions

*What are good choices of protein?*

Skinless chicken, fish (especially oily fish), skinless turkey, veal, pulses, Quorn, eggs, nuts and seeds. Try to stay away from: bacon, sausages, beef, lamb, ham, duck, goose, pheasant and salami.

*My energy drops mid-morning and mid-afternoon. I have a cup of coffee and a biscuit but I am hungry again quickly. How can I stop this?*

This is the insulin rollercoaster I mentioned earlier. When you have a cup of coffee and a biscuit you are putting lots of sugar into your bloodstream. They are converted very quickly into sugar and quickly leave your body again. To stop this change your coffee and biscuit snack! You need to make sure you eat low GI snacks to balance your blood sugar throughout the day and to manage your hunger. Try any of the snacks mentioned above. That should help. Also make sure you eat every 3-4 hours. If you leave it longer, you will get a crash in blood sugar and crave something sweet to pick you up.

*I want to move away from eating bread at lunchtime but don't know what I could eat instead. Any ideas?*

It is quite hard to find something for lunch when you are out and about that doesn't involve bread. The key here is forward planning. Make your lunch and take it with you. That way you can choose what you eat. There are many alternatives to bread based lunches. For example, try soup, stir fry with noodles/rice, pasta with vegetables or salad, a hearty salad with protein and fish with rice and vegetables. All of these options are healthy and well balanced. Make sure you have 20% starchy complex carbohydrates (choose something other than bread), 40% complex carbohydrates and 40% protein for lunch. That way you will be sure to have lasting energy and a feeling of fullness well into the afternoon.

### I have heard about the 5:2 fasting diet. What do you think to this?

I am not a fan of any 'diet'. I would recommend you focus on eating a healthy balanced diet and living by the 80-20 rule. Many 'diets' restrict intake and this isn't good on the body. The 5:2 diet falls into this category. It encourages 'dieting' for 2 days of the week and eating whatever you like on the 5 days. It doesn't give any thought to calorie control on the 5 days, which means you can literally eat anything. I don't see this way of eating sustainable and would encourage you instead to tweak your existing eating habits.

# Chapter 9: Store Cupboard Essentials

We all have a store cupboard, right? Have a look in yours right now. What do you see?

Do you see a random selection of items or do you see essential ingredients for different meals?

Think about stocking up your store cupboard so you can reach in and make a meal up from scratch without much effort. If you forward plan and know what ingredients are good in what dishes, you will have a better chance of making something magical in the kitchen.

Here are the essential ingredients I always keep in, for those magical moments.

## Grains
- Brown rice
- Good quality dried pastas and noodles (buckwheat noodles, rice, egg)
- Couscous
- Breakfast cereal - oat flakes etc
- Quinoa
- Rye/whole grain bread
- Wholemeal pitta bread
- Oatcakes
- Ryvita
- Corn cakes

## Pulses
- Canned butter beans
- Canned cannellini beans
- Canned chick peas
- Canned flageolet beans

- Canned baked beans
- Lentils - red, green and Puy (canned or dried)
- Canned mixed beans
- Canned red kidney beans
- Dried split yellow lentils

**Nuts and Seeds**

- Cashew nuts (not honey or salted!)
- Hazelnuts
- Linseeds
- Pine nuts
- Pumpkin seeds
- Sesame seeds
- Sunflower seeds
- Walnuts
- Almonds
- Pecans
- Nut and seed butters (good quality)

**Oils**

- Extra virgin olive oil
- Sesame oil
- Walnut oil
- Rapeseed oil
- Avocado oil
- Coconut oil

**Herbs (fresh or dried)**

- Basil
- Bay leaves
- Chives
- Coriander
- Dill

- Fennel
- Lemongrass
- Mint
- Mixed herbs (dried)
- Oregano (dried)
- Parsley
- Rosemary
- Sage
- Thyme

**Spices**
- Black pepper
- Cayenne
- Chilli powder
- Fresh chillies
- Ground cinnamon
- Ground coriander
- Cumin seeds
- Cardamom pods
- Curry powder
- Fennel seeds
- Five spice
- Garlic (dried and fresh)
- Garam Masala
- Ginger (fresh)
- Kalonji seeds (fabulous in scrambled eggs)
- Black mustard seeds
- Nutmeg (amazing in lasagne)
- Onion powder
- Paprika
- Poppy seeds
- Salt
- Tamarind paste

- Turmeric

## Sauces

- Horseradish sauce
- Mustards - Dijon, whole grain
- Soy sauce
- Fish stock
- Vegetable stock
- Thai fish sauce
- Tomato puree
- Vinegars - balsamic, white wine, cider
- Worchester sauce

## Dried Fruits

- Apricots
- Currants
- Cranberries
- Figs
- Apples
- Mangos
- Prunes
- Raisins
- Sultanas

## Others

- Tinned tomatoes
- Honey
- Jam
- Marmalade
- Tinned anchovy fillets
- Tinned mackerel
- Tinned tuna (dolphin friendly)
- Tinned salmon

- Tinned sardines
- Teas - green, camomile, fruit
- Dark chocolate
- Pesto and olive pastes
- Sundried tomatoes (in oil or dried)

It is guaranteed that if you have some or all of these in your store cupboard, you can only cook up a storm in the kitchen!

## Over to You

Go and take a look right now in your cupboards. What can you chuck out (look at dates as a starting point) and what can you introduce to your cupboards to make meal times a bit more exciting and healthy?

# Chapter 10: The Essential Ingredients for Healthy Meals

Here are my essential ingredients to create healthy meals. Choose the ones you like, mix them up and try them out. Aim for the proportions of carbohydrates, protein and fats as talked about earlier. I have detailed some of the core families so that you can think about what to buy in fresh. I haven't included again the ingredients I have mentioned in the previous pages.

**Seasonal vegetables:** Red, green, orange, yellow, purple, brown, white. Keep it colourful! Aubergines, beansprouts, beetroot, broccoli, cabbage, carrots, celery, Chinese leaves, corn, courgettes, green beans, leeks, mangetout, mushrooms, onions, parsnips, peas, chillies, shallots, sprouted seeds, butternut squash, sugar snap peas, swedes, sweet potatoes.

**Seasonal fresh fruits:** Apples, blackberries, blueberries, grapefruit, kiwi fruit, lemons, limes, oranges, pears, raspberries. Again, keep it colourful!

**Salad stuff:** Avocados, cucumbers, lettuce - romaine or cos, mixed salad leaves, sweet peppers, rocket, spinach, tomatoes, watercress, spring onions, radishes, fresh herbs - parsley, chives, basil.

**Grains:** Oat flakes, barley flakes, bran flakes, buckwheat flakes, sugar free cereal, millet, rye flakes, rye bread, whole grain bread, porridge, muesli, whole-wheat pasta, whole grain bread, brown rice, pitta pockets, rye bread, pumpernickel bread, whole grain tortilla.

**Proteins:**
**Poultry** - Skinless chicken breasts, turkey.
**Oily fish** - mackerel, sardines, salmon, herring, kippers, anchovies, fresh tuna, swordfish, trout, whitebait.

**Other fish and shellfish** - prawns etc.
**Tofu**.
**Pulses** - beans, lentils, peas.
**Nuts and seeds**.

**Milk and dairy products:** low fat, skimmed and semi-skimmed milk, butter, cottage cheese, crème fraiche, live natural yoghurt, cheeses (feta, hard and soft goats cheese, parmesan cheese).
**Eggs** - organic and free range. Hens, quails.

**Dips and spreads**: houmous, tzatziki, salsa, tahini and guacamole.

I hope this gives you some foods that you haven't thought about previously and inspires you to try out new foods and combinations.

## Over to You

Which foods haven't you tried before that you would like to give a go? Make a list and a plan on how you will introduce a few new foods into your diet this week.

## Quiz - How Healthy Are You?

Try out this quiz to see how healthy you are. Be honest and go with your gut instinct.

**I choose:**
a. Foods that are fast, quick and easy to eat on the go
b. Foods that make me feel full quickly
c. Fresh, homemade foods

**I eat:**
a. Very quickly and on the go
b. Quickly but sat down
c. Slowly and carefully, enjoying the food

**I think:**
a. Food just keeps me going
b. Food makes me feel full and have energy
c. Food is sacred and nourishes me to ensure that I can do everything I want

**I eat out:**
a. More often than 3 times a week or order in takeaways
b. A couple of times a week
c. Once a week or less

**How many portions of fruit and vegetables do you eat each day?**
a. 0
b. 1 - 3
c. 4+

**What do you choose to snack on during the day?**
a. A chocolate bar, crisps and coffee
b. A cup of tea and a homemade cookie
c. A glass of water with a piece of fruit and a small handful of nuts

**When you eat protein, what do you choose?**
a. Red meats such as steak, sausages and burgers
b. I don't eat meat. I eat pulses
c. Poultry, lean meat and fish

**What do you choose for lunch?**
a. Sausage roll, pastries, a premade sandwich or something quick I can grab at the shop
b. Jacket potato with cheese
c. I prepare my lunch at home and have a rice based salad with chicken, a sandwich on whole-wheat bread or soup with a wedge of whole-wheat bread

**You are running late in the morning. You haven't eaten breakfast yet. What do you do?**
a. Skip it. You regularly do
b. Make white toast with jam and eat on the run
c. Make time for whole grain cereal with skimmed milk and chopped fruit

**When you grab a drink on the go, what do you opt for?**
a. A fizzy drink
b. A shop bought smoothie
c. A bottle of water

**How many glasses of water do you drink per day?**
a. None
b. 1 - 4
c. 5 - 8

**How much of your diet consists of whole grains, vegetables, fruit, fish, lean meat and dairy versus how much consists of junk food?**
a. I try and eat healthily but my life is so busy that I usually skip meals and grab on the go
b. I eat well enough but have a tendency to eat too much or snack on bad foods

c.  I follow a healthy, nutritionally balanced diet which consists of lots of colour and variety day to day

**Do you:**
a.  Skip meals on a regular basis
b.  Skip meals 2 - 4 times a week
c.  Always eat 3 meals a day and snack healthily

**Do you:**
a.  Finish your meals off and start snacking within 30 minutes even if you still feel full
b.  Have to finish off every meal, even though you feel uncomfortably full
c.  Know when you have had enough and sometimes leave food on your plate

**Now, total up how many a's, b's and c's you have.**

**A = not healthy.** Read back through this section and identify the top 3 things you can change right now, that will be easy and painless for you. Make these changes right now. Consider eating regularly and not skipping meals, lowering your alcohol and coffee intake, eating more fruit and vegetables and drinking more water. Also think about changing your attitude towards food. It is there to nourish your body and by putting in the wrong nutrients regularly, you are encouraging health complications for your future.

**B = getting there.** You have a good idea of what it means to be healthy. You now need to tweak what you are doing to make sure you are eating a variety of foods each day in the correct proportions. Read up on portion sizes and the how to eat section. Also, educate yourself on what are the best choices of foods e.g. whole-wheat instead of white. Ensure you are eating the right balance of fats and getting in your fruit and vegetables every day.

**C = healthy and happy.** You are healthy. This is great and you are sure to be noticing the energy that you have, the vibrancy of your skin and that you are maintaining a healthy, sustainable weight. Share your knowledge with those around you and help them to understand how to make simple changes with their eating habits and intake. See if there is anything in your diet that could be improved further. Maybe look at making your own sauces and dressings from scratch (don't buy pre-made ones) or cutting out trans fats and processed meats completely.

## Summary Section 2

We have taken a whistle stop tour at the foods you should and shouldn't be eating in your diet. There is a lot to take in with this. Let me reiterate here that you don't need to understand all the science to get the benefit from this information. Take a look at the tips and the summaries and think about how you can tweak a few things in your diet right now to make it healthier. Below are the key things you need to remember and the 3 exercises we explored in the section.

## Things to Remember

### Know What Foods Count as Healthy Options
- Simple carbohydrates
- Complex carbohydrates (unrefined)
- Complete & incomplete proteins
- Fats
- Vitamins and minerals
- Drinks

### Cut Out the Unhealthy
- Simple carbohydrates
- Complex carbohydrates (refined)
- Proteins
- Trans Fats

### Actions to Explore
- Eliminate the Core 5 to avoid insulin production
- Choose low GI carbohydrates
- Be aware of the sugar alternatives and refined sugars that you need to stay away from
- Get the right balance of animal and non-animal proteins in your diet

- Get the right balance of unsaturated and unsaturated fats in your diet
- Live by the 80-20 rule
- Know how to measure a portion
- Make sure you have the right proportions of carbohydrates, protein and fat on your plate
- The listed exercises
- Come up with new ideas for meals and snacks that are healthy and balanced
- Sort out your store cupboard. Chuck out, clean out and magic it up
- New food experimentation. Try out new foods and combinations

# Part 2:
# Everything You Need to Know About Exercise

# Chapter 11: Introduction to Exercise

Some people think of exercise as something that has to be fitted in to life and is a chore. Other people think of exercise as something that will help them to manage their stress levels and will give them more energy throughout the day.

It is well documented that exercise helps to manage stress levels, keeps you in good health and increases the 'feel good' hormones. Integrated into a healthy lifestyle, exercise will help you to feel on top of your game.

Think of Christmas Day. It is a common occurrence for a family to sit and eat all day. There isn't much exercise that takes place in between all of the festive eating. The next day you feel flabby and bloated. As soon as you get out in to the fresh air and get active (whatever that may involve) you start to feel better. You feel lighter and like everything is moving around as it should inside. Does this sound familiar?

Getting active can have a massive impact on your body, mind and emotions. It can clear your head, help you to put things into perspective, help you to lose weight and help you to improve your fitness levels and overall health.

In this section we will look at the different types of exercise, why it is important to stay active and how to build it into your everyday life. Let's face it; if it's not integrated into your current lifestyle and responsibilities it won't happen. Let's look at how you can embed it into your life so you can feel on top of your game.

## Importance of Activity

Being active is important to maintaining a healthy and happier life. People who lead an active life are less likely to get ill and more likely to live longer. Exercise not only makes you physically fitter, it also improves your mental health and general sense of wellbeing.

There are many benefits of exercising and keeping active.

Here are a few of the key ones:

- It improves your fitness, strength and flexibility
- It improves your breathing and lung capacity
- It will help to maintain a healthy and sustainable weight
- It speeds up your metabolism
- It increases your energy levels
- It increases the 'feel good' hormones in your body
- It helps to deal with stress more effectively
- It strengthens your muscles and organs
- It improves your sleep
- It improves circulation and lowers blood pressure
- It can clear your mind
- It will give you time and space away from everything to think and be quiet
- It allows you the time to put things into perspective and weigh up options
- It will get you outdoors breathing in the fresh air
- It will get you in tune with nature

So what happens if you don't exercise? Physically and mentally, you will experience the reverse of all the key benefits mentioned above. You may also feel run down, low in mood and unsociable.

Medically, there is an increased risk of type 2 diabetes, osteoporosis (bone loss), heart attack, stroke and high blood pressure (amongst other things).

So why wouldn't you want to keep active and look after your body, mind and spirit?

Keeping active doesn't need to be painful, time consuming or something to dread. If you have the right attitude about it, it can be fun, enjoyable and something you look forward to.

## Summary

- Being active is fundamental to achieving good health and wellbeing.
- There are many health benefits to being active.
- If you don't keep fit and active, you will notice health issues cropping up over time.

# Chapter 12: Barriers to Exercise

What is it that stops you from exercising? There are many reasons people don't exercise or stop themselves from getting active every day. Here I detail the main ones my clients have told me over the years.

**Time.** This is the biggest reason people don't exercise. It is a common thought that exercising takes a lot of time out of your day. It is also a common thought that it stops you from doing something else that is more important. Think about this: what is more important than looking after your health and wellbeing?

**Family commitments.** Many people have families, whether young or older. Looking after family can take time out of your day, can use up your energies and test your nerves at times. Finding the time in the day to build in activity will help you to deal with your commitments, be more productive and have better relationships with your loved ones.

**Appearance.** Some people are worried about how they look when they exercise or get active. You may think you look too sweaty or that you need the most expensive exercise equipment and clothing. This can stop you from even starting. You don't need the best gear on the market to get active and you are not alone when you sweat during exercise!

**"I need money to exercise."** Some people think they need to have money to access the local gym or to buy equipment to exercise. Money shouldn't be a barrier to getting active. There are many things you can do every day to be more active and to feel the benefits this can bring. I will discuss these in detail later in the chapter.

**Overweight.** Some people think that they are too overweight to get active and to exercise. Your weight may stop you from wanting to exercise in front of others who you feel may appear more toned and fitter than you are. Your weight itself may restrict movement or activities that you can engage in. The key is to find something you can do and to build up slowly.

**Aches and pains.** When your body hurts, or you feel ill you may be less inclined to exercise. You may feel pain when you move and feel that you shouldn't exercise 'just in case'. Provided there are no medical issues or physical injuries, getting active could help to manage your pain and will help you to feel healthier. If you are unsure, ask your GP.

**Motivation.** It is easy to get home from work and think, "I can't be bothered" either to go back out or to do something physical. Some days you may feel like you just don't want to get active. Guy, a client wanting to improve his fitness, regularly found that he felt this way after a busy day in the office. To deal with this, he used to tell himself that it was a temporary thought. He always felt great when he started the exercise and realised that it gave him so much more energy when he did. When the thoughts kicked in, he would bat them away, get his workout clothes on and just get on with it.

**Illness or injury** can cause you to think that you can't do any type of exercise at all. Vicki, a hairdresser, had an injury when she was younger. She hurt her leg while running which has stopped her from doing any type of exercise or activity ever since. She put on 3 stone over the years and felt very sluggish and tired most of the time. She stopped herself from doing any exercise ever since. When I asked her what she liked to do, she said she loved swimming and walking the dog when she was younger. She hasn't done these things in years. When I asked her if she felt she could do these things now, she said her leg doesn't hurt when she does certain activities but she has a fear that it may hurt. This fear has stopped her from doing anything. She felt she could swim and walk the dog now. She decided from this point on that she wouldn't fear anything going forwards and would try to be more active.

Some illnesses do stop people from getting active. Whatever the illness or injury, think of all the things you CAN do. Focus on these and do them instead of thinking about the things you can't do. There are virtually no medical conditions that will keep you from doing any type of exercise. Consult with your GP if you are not sure but try to find something that you can do and build it up slowly.

**Inconvenient location.** Working away from home or not being near to a gym is a common barrier to exercising. Do you need to be near a gym? Can you be active when you are away from home? What could you do to be active where you are?

So those are a few of the reasons why people don't get active. Which ones of those do you use as excuses and barriers to exercising?

I mentioned earlier that having the right attitude to being active was the key.

Think of getting active as a way to look after your health and wellbeing. If you don't look after your health and wellbeing, your body will not operate on full power. Being fit and healthy ensures you can think clearly and will avoid you getting bugs in your body. It is the way to ensure you can do everything you want to do and achieve all of your goals. Invest in the time to get active, to move about and to look after your health.

## Summary

 There are many barriers that you can come up with to excuse not exercising.

- Having the right attitude to exercise is the key to integrating it into your daily life.
- Identify your barriers to exercise and work around these.

# Chapter 13: The Basics

A common question I get asked is 'how much activity should I do?' The recommended time is 20 minutes at least 3 times a week. However, I tell people to do as much as you feel you can. If you are restricted by your weight or an illness, you may not be able to do as much as someone who is a little fitter and doesn't have an illness. Your body knows how much it can deal with. If you feel in pain at any time or don't feel well, stop.

Most of my clients think at first that you have to do the recommended 20 minutes all at once. This is not the case. If you want to increase your activity levels, every little bit counts. You could split the 20 minutes into two 10-minute blocks or four 5-minute blocks. I recommend doing something every day for at least 20 minutes. If you can fit in more and feel able to do so, then go for it. If you can't manage the 20 minutes, still do something. 5 minutes is better than nothing. You can start to build it up to the 20 minutes over time.

A common misconception is that you can do a really long workout and that will 'last you' all week. Fitness doesn't work like that. You need to do something to keep active little and often. A 20 minute workout every day will be far more productive and beneficial than a 2 hour bike ride once a month.

One of my clients, Simon, wanted to lose 4 stone. He was a quite big guy at the time that we started working together. He told me that he was really fit and regularly exercised. He loved cycling and told me he ate well around his exercise. He had been cycling for nearly a year but was not losing any weight. He was starting to become disheartened by it all. When we delved into his exercise habits and routines, it was obvious why he wasn't losing any weight.

First of all, he cycled once a month. He would cycle very impressive distances in this one long day. He didn't do any other activity in the month. This was the first thing he needed to address. Only being active one day in the month would not encourage weight loss, regardless of the distance covered.

When we started looking into his eating around this day of cycling, there were a few things that stood out that were not working for him. He would take chocolate with him to snack on all day. When he got tired he would have a chocolate bar. He would drink a commercial energy drink pre, during and post exercise. At lunchtime he would stop at a pub and eat a big (unhealthy) lunch and wash it down with a few pints. When he got home he would eat something equally as unhealthy and wash it down with more pints or wine. He thought that because he had cycled so far and burnt x number of calories that he could eat whatever he wanted to.

All of these things in combination were not working for him. Your body is very receptive to what you feed it pre, during and post exercise. Giving his body this kind of food was hindering the weight loss he wanted to see. Making a few changes to this routine made a massive difference for Simon. He lost the 4 stone easily and continues to lose weight to reach his longer-term goal.

Regular exercise is the key. Your exercise doesn't have to be vigorous either. You can find ways to fit being active into your daily routine.

Let us look now at the main types of exercise. There are three main types that you will be familiar with: aerobic exercise, resistance exercise and flexibility exercise.

If you want a healthy heart, you are recommended to do some aerobic exercise (also known as cardio). These are activities that use oxygen, raise your heart rate and make you slightly out of breath. This type of exercise keeps your heart, lungs, muscles and blood vessels healthy and it improves your fitness levels.

I am often asked to clarify what counts as aerobic. Here are some ideas:

- **Walking.** If you're just starting out with exercise, this is a good place to start.
- **Cycling.** Great for improving fitness and helps to strengthen your upper leg muscles. It also helps with balance! Very good for leg tone in general.
- **Swimming.** Your whole body is involved in this exercise and it doesn't stress your joints. Good for people who have mobility issues and people that are just starting out.
- **Aerobics.** This involves routines of exercises to music. You generally have an instructor that guides you through and will help to make the workout fun. Classes are run at most sports centres, gyms etc. These are a good way to be social and to exercise at the same time.
- **Running.** Burns more calories than walking and improves your fitness. The world is your oyster with this one!
- **Team sports**, such as football, netball, hockey. A good way to stay motivated because the whole team is relying on you and supports each other. Also a good social activity.

Resistance exercise increases your strength. This kind of activity will give your body a more toned look and may help to improve your posture. Engaging in resistance exercise helps to build more muscle. Muscle burns more calories than fat tissue, even when you are at rest. Building muscle will help you to stay a healthy weight. If you are aiming to maintain a healthy and sustainable weight, you want to make sure you are doing some resistance exercises regularly, at least two or three times a week.

So how do you do strength training? You can use your own body weight (which involves no cost), free weights (such as dumbbells), rubber bands or weight lifting machines (commonly seen in gyms). Aim to work all of your major muscle groups in your body. Find the right level or weight that allows you to do a set of 8 to 12 repetitions at a time. Try to do 3 - 4 sets with each muscle group.

Most people think they have to join a gym to engage in strength training. This is not the case. You can lift weights at home, using everyday items in the house as the weight. You can use your own body weight, e.g. chair dips. Household activities also count, for example carrying shopping, gardening. Try to plan it so you have a rest day in between strength training. This will allow your muscles to repair and build in between sessions.

Flexibility exercises help to stretch your muscles. If you don't regularly stretch them, they are at risk of becoming shorter and less elastic. This reduces your movement in joints and increases stiffness and risk of injuries. You should aim to do some flexibility exercises for a few minutes every day.

Yoga, pilates and tai chi include many exercises that focus on suppleness and flexibility. You will gently ease and stretch your body into different positions and then hold these while concentrating on your breathing. This will also help you to relax, improve your balance, posture and circulation.

## Frequently Asked Questions

*I haven't exercised for quite a while. How should I start?*

If you haven't exercised for a while, start gently and gradually increase your effort level and time. As you get fitter, you will need to work harder to feel breathless and raise your heart rate.

Choose an activity that you can do that will fit in around your day. You are more likely to continue it if you do that. Choose something you like to do, otherwise you will resent it.

Set yourself some goals. This will motivate you to continue and will show you how you are progressing. So if for instance, you are able to engage in 10 minutes at a time, your goal may be to keep the same speed and intensity and do it for 12 minutes. Keep your goals realistic, achievable and short term. This will keep your spirits up, enable you to see progress quickly and lift you when you have achieved them.

Also consider tracking your activity throughout the week. This will show you how much you have done and make sure you are keeping to your target. There are many ways to do this. You could use an app on your phone, computer or iPod. You can draw up an activity chart and stick it on the wall. Mark on what you have done and when. You could email yourself every time you have done something. Create a folder and put the email in the folder to remind you.

Keep going. Even if you don't feel like doing any exercise today or this week, make yourself do it. You will feel better afterwards and happier that you did something.

*I like to exercise but don't tend to do it because I am tired when I get in. What can I do?*

Try to find something you can do during the day that will fit in around what you are doing. So it may be walking to work, to the shops etc. It may be playing with the kids in the garden. Whatever it is, try to fit it in to your daily routine. Exercise doesn't need to be something you do when you get home.

It may motivate you more if you team up with a friend, partner or colleague. Find something that you both like to do and support each other to do it. Sometimes it is easier to get into a new activity if you have someone that you are accountable to. If you say you are going to exercise to someone else, it may spur you on to do it.

I have two friends who really wanted to be active but found every excuse going to not do it. They regularly told me that they would be going running on a certain day but would come back and say they hadn't gone because of 'insert reason here'. They would then say they really, really wanted to get back into it. One day they decided to make a commitment to each other to go running every Saturday first thing in the morning. For the first few weeks, they really didn't look forward to it. They soon got into the habit of it and slowly built up their fitness levels. Now, they still go running every Saturday and have committed to running a half marathon. Sometimes, you may need a bit of encouragement and accountability. It has worked wonders for my two friends. If you identify with this, it might be worth finding an exercise partner!

## What is interval training?

Interval training (also known as HIIT – high intensity interval training) involves alternating bursts of intense activity with intervals of less intense or lighter activity. For example, if you are on an indoor bike, you would do a few minutes warm up cycling. Then you would do a very fast 30 seconds (for example) peddling as fast as you can. When the 30 seconds is over, you would drop to cycling much slower for 2 minutes (for example). You would alternate the fast bursts of 30 seconds with the slower 2-minute blocks for the duration of your workout. You can do this with any activity you are doing; walking, running and swimming. All you do is introduce faster bursts for a certain length of time into your activity.

### What is the point with interval training?

The idea with interval training is that it works your body much harder. During the high intensity phase, your body burns mainly carbohydrates (for energy) but during the recovery, your body burns mainly fat (to produce the energy needed to help the body recover). This process can continue for hours after the exercise has finished, which can help you to lose weight, provided you are eating healthily.

The fast and slow pattern trains your body to recover quickly which will gradually increase your ability to run/swim/cycle faster for longer.

### How often should I interval train?

Because of the intensity of the exercise involved here, don't try to do this every time you exercise. Maybe once or twice a week would be good.

## Summary

- There are 3 main types of exercise: aerobic exercise, resistance exercise and flexibility exercise.
- Do as much as you feel you are able to.

- 💜 Do something every day for at least 20 minutes.
- 💜 You can split the 20 minutes down into more manageable chunks.
- 💜 If you are in pain or feel unwell, stop.
- 💜 Regular exercise is the key.
- 💜 Exercise doesn't need to be vigorous.
- 💜 You can find ways to fit being active into your daily routine.
- 💜 Consider finding an exercise partner.
- 💜 HIIT will help you to lose weight.

# Chapter 14: How to Begin

Here are my top tips and things to think about on how to start being more active and fitting exercise into your daily life. Remember, you don't need a gym!

Do something every day. Whatever it is, just do something.

Think of what you do during the day. How can you fit some form of activity or exercise into this? For example, do you work close to home? If so, could you walk instead of using the car? Do you have meetings at work that last for a while? Could you ask to have a walking meeting instead? Do you have children and drive them to school, the shops or activities? Could you make it more fun for them and bring in activity to this schedule? Maybe walk them to where you are going or take a football with you?

What times in the day are you inactive? Could you do something to build activity into it? For example, do you sit and watch TV when you get in from work? Could you do something like strength training whilst watching TV? Or could you go out for a brisk walk, run or cycle ride instead?

Think of all the cardio activities you can do during your daily routines. Here are a few ideas:

How about walking, cycling (great to get to places quickly), running, jogging or hill walking?

Think about how to get the kids involved too. Try swimming, skipping, playing football, playing badminton, swingball, hopscotch, chase and dancing. Kids love to do all of these and they will get your heart rate up and start to get you breathless!

How about vacuuming, mowing the lawn, cleaning the house (floors, windows), gardening, yard cleaning, sweeping, weeding or washing and polishing the car? The added bonus is you will have a nice clean house too!

Want to do a routine at home that is more energetic? Try squats, jumping jacks, step ups on the stairs, star jumps, burpees, lunges. The list is endless. There are many fantastic workouts posted on YouTube. Why not get on and have a look for a home workout?

Think of the resistance training you can do at home. Lifting objects - such as bags of sugar, tins of beans, push ups (you can make these easier or harder for yourself), tricep dips, shoulder presses (you need a rubber band for this one), squats, stomach crunches and free weights if you want to lift weights. The gardening is a great one for this too. Again, take a look on YouTube for workouts to tone and strengthen your muscles.

**Other Ideas**
- Explore your surroundings. Walk, run, jog, cycle. Get outside and enjoy what is all around you. Listen to the birds tweeting and the sound of the wind in the trees. Even if it is cold, wrap up warm and get outside. You will see some amazing sights and feel more relaxed.
- Park further away from the office or get off the bus one stop earlier.
- Choose the stairs.
- Drink more water – you will need to go to the toilet more.
- Walk instead of getting the bus or using the car.
- Spend less time sat down. Get on your feet. Get out of the chair and walk across the office. Walk around whilst talking on the phone.
- Carry your shopping to the car. It will tone your arms.

- Find an active hobby that you can enjoy, such as swimming and dancing.

You can see there are many activities you can engage in that don't involve paying a gym membership. And the benefit of these activities is that they are free, get you out in the fresh air, give you quality family and friend time and keep you active!

Remember the key is to engage in activity regularly throughout the week. Find new ways to be active every day — at home, work or in leisure. If you can build it into your daily life, you will find it so much easier to increase your activity levels and to sustain it throughout your life.

Think now about what you currently do? Are you active? Could you do more? What could you do to build more activity into your life? Who could you engage with to make it more fun and enjoyable?

**Be Aware**
There are a few things to be aware of when exercising. Here are the 5 main ones.

People think they can exercise once a week for a long period of time and that will make up for not being active the rest of the week. Your body will not thank you for doing this to it. It will put strain on your body, will make you more prone to injury and will not increase your fitness levels or help to lose weight. You need to make sure you are active every day. This will increase your fitness and give you all the health benefits that are associated with exercise and activity.

Many people don't eat before they exercise. They think that it will help them to lose weight if they don't eat. If you do this, you are not fuelling up and giving your body the energy and nutrients it needs to function properly. This will not help you to lose weight. It may trigger the starvation response instead, which will make your body hold on to all the food you put in to your body. This will make you put weight on in the longer term. It could also mean you don't have enough energy to complete your workout.

Just as people don't eat before they exercise, many people don't eat afterwards. This is equally as bad as not eating before it. Your body is restricted of nutrients it is craving post exercise. You will have used glycogen (stored energy) and will have free radicals in your body as a result of the exercise. Your body needs to replace its energy that it has used up and needs antioxidants to combat and neutralise the free radicals.

You need to feed your body post exercise to ensure you are giving it what it needs to recover, repair and function properly. I will talk about pre and post exercise food in the next section.

People think they can eat junk food straight after exercise since they just burned x number of calories. Your body has a half an hour window (approximately) post exercise where it is more sensitive to the effects of insulin. This is the optimum time to replace lost glycogen and to get good quality, healthy food into your body. If you put in a chocolate cream egg (or something equally as unhealthy) in the 30-minute window, the nutrients will go straight into your stores to replace the energy you have lost. Do you really want to be putting in junk food during this time? Anything you put in during this time will be stored for energy for use in the future.

Not stretching before and after exercise will cause injuries. It is really important that you stretch your muscles before starting and after exercise. This warms and stretches your muscles so they won't be shocked when you start! You also need to make sure you warm up properly and cool down after exercise. You really don't want to be shocking your body and making it work too hard too quickly. This can cause injury and illness.

Make sure you are aware of these 5 common misconceptions and think about what you do now. If you do any of these, try to break the habit and do something different.

We will look in the next pages about how to eat well for exercise and how to make sure you are giving your body what it needs.

## Summary

- Do something every day.
- Look at what you do now and how you can build more activity into your day.
- Engage in cardio, strength training and flexibility exercises.
- You don't need to join a gym to be active!
- Identify what you do now. Could you do more? What times of day are you inactive?
- What could you do to fit more activity into your day?

## Chapter 15: Sports Nutrition

The connection between food and exercise is sometimes forgotten. You need to make sure you eat well for fitness. Do you think about the food you eat and how it impacts on your body when it comes to exercise? You wouldn't be alone if you overlook this.

In this section we will look at how to fuel up, how to look after yourself during and how to repair quickly and effectively afterwards. Food is a fundamental part to this process so we will be looking at the kind of things you should be eating around exercise.

Why do this? If you get it right, you will allow your metabolism to run efficiently, you will have peak physical performance and maintain your focus and concentration.

It is crucial to fuel and repair your body before, during and after exercise. Most people don't do this and that is why they have a slower recovery rate, feel tired and have no energy. If you do this correctly, you can cut down on recovery time whilst ensuring your body is repairing fully. You can also maximise the energy you have and give greater performance whilst engaging in the exercise itself.

When you exercise you run down your energy stores (glycogen) and lose essential salts and minerals (known as electrolytes) through perspiration. You also increase the free radicals within your body. Free radicals are responsible for aging, tissue damage and possibly some diseases.

Antioxidants, present in many foods, are molecules that prevent free radicals from harming the healthy tissue in your body.

So what do you need to fuel the body correctly? You need to eat carbohydrates to fuel the engine, protein to repair and construct, fat to help move nutrients around, vitamins and minerals to give efficiency and antioxidants to combat the free radicals that are produced by exercise.

There are 5 stages to eating well around fitness. These are the Fuel Up, In-Activity, Top Up, Mend and Recover stages. A handy acronym to help remember this is: FIT-MR(S). The S is just for effect… You need to make sure you are taking into account all these stages to ensure you are properly fuelling your body. We will look at each of these stages in turn now.

## Fuel Up Stage

This should take place around 30-60 minutes before exercising. Here you need to focus on eating complex carbohydrates; the lower the GI the better. Eating complex carbohydrates will avoid the rapid rise in blood glucose and insulin. Aim to have foods low in fibre, low in fat and low in protein. Protein takes a long time to digest so will just sit unprocessed in your stomach while you exercise. This will give you a stitch and cramps.

## In-Activity Stage

Hydrate! If you lose 5% of your body fluid, this impacts by 30% on your aerobic capacity. You will notice a massive difference with your performance. Don't forget that your stomach shuts down in exercise and if you have undigested food in your stomach you will experience cramps or a sick feeling.

If your activity or event is over an hour in duration, refuel every hour. Eat carbohydrates during the event if the session is longer than 1 hour, the match or race is longer than 90 minutes and/or if a pre exercise meal is not possible. You can do this through drinking isotonic drinks if it is not possible with food.

You need to make sure you replenish with carbohydrates, water and electrolytes to top up what has been lost during the exercise. Isotonic drinks are a good way to get these.

**Top Up Stage**

When you exercise you use up the glycogen you have stored in your liver and muscles. When you have finished exercising you need to refill these stores. There is a 30-minute window after exercise where your muscles are more sensitive to the effects of insulin. During this time your body enables a more efficient replacement of lost glycogen. To restore the glycogen in the body you need to eat good quality carbohydrates and protein. This will start the repair work on your muscles.

**Mend Stage**

Roughly 1.5-2 hours after exercise, you need to consume high quality protein. This ensures the repair process continues and decreases the injury risk in the next session. You also need to eat low GI carbohydrates at this stage. A good idea is to have a balanced, healthy meal. This is the easiest way to get in all the nutrients you need post exercise.

A note on muscles. When you exercise you damage the muscles and tissues in your body. If you don't eat protein (which helps to repair and construct muscle tissue) after exercise, your body will break down other muscles in your body so it can fix the ones that have been damaged. Energy is used in this process. You need to feed your body protein approximately every 2 hours to ensure you are building quicker than you are breaking down the muscles. Muscles repair faster and are greatly improved if you refuel and repair properly.

**Recover Stage**

This takes place around 48-72 hours after exercise has taken place. You need to consume antioxidants during this time.

This will combat and neutralise the free radicals in your body created by strenuous activity.

## IDEAS ON WHAT TO EAT

**Pre-Exercise**
- Wholemeal spaghetti, rice, pasta
- Whole-wheat bread with jam
- Houmous with raw vegetable sticks
- Oatmeal/whole grain crackers with nut butter, low fat cottage cheese or cheese
- Nuts and raisins
- Most vegetables
- Fresh fruits: pineapple, apricots, banana, mango
- Milk or low fat yoghurt

**During:** isotonic drinks (see note below).

**Immediately After**
- Rice cakes with nut butter
- Watermelon
- Dates
- Bread or English muffin with peanut butter
- Yoghurt with fruit
- Fruit juice with cheese
- Eggs and toast
- Turkey, ham or roast beef sandwich
- Chocolate milk
- Fruit smoothie

**Repair:** healthy, balanced meal with carbohydrates, protein and fats. Keep topping up with protein through snacks every 2-3 hours.

**Recovery:** lots of fresh fruit and vegetables.

**Isotonic Drinks**

Isotonic drinks are designed to quickly replace the fluids which are lost through perspiration. They also provide carbohydrates, in the concentrated form of glucose and salts and minerals similar to those you would find in your body.

Glucose from the drink is drawn quickly into the blood. As a result, isotonics contribute towards hydration. Isotonic drinks are most useful during activity, rather than pre or post workout.

I have a number of concerns around isotonic drinks. The products need to stand out and be marketable in a highly competitive market. To stand out they usually contain strong colourings and various processed sugars are added to provide energy. Sweeteners such as Aspartame, Acesulfame K and Saccharin are often added. I talked about these sweeteners earlier and we explored the health issues that are linked to them. Commercial sports drinks usually contain artificial flavourings. They are not a healthy choice in my eyes and are linked to weight gain.

A client, Paul, came to see me who cycles a fair bit. He used isotonics post exercise to give him some energy. He put on a considerable amount of weight when he introduced it into his routine. His body was getting too much simple sugar and was being shifted by insulin into the fat stores. He cut isotonics out as a result of our sessions and started to see the difference in his appearance as well as his physical ability whilst cycling.

Isotonic drinks are designed to replenish water, carbohydrates and electrolytes that are lost during exercise. It is a good idea to replace these to ensure optimum performance. As I mentioned earlier, I don't see the commercial isotonics as a healthy option and I would discourage you from wasting your money on them. Instead, here are two natural options you could try instead.

1.  Mix 500ml of pure, unsweetened fruit juice with 500ml of water and add 1/5 teaspoon of natural, unprocessed salt
2.  Dilute 60g pure glucose in 1 litre of water and add 1/5 teaspoon of natural, unprocessed salt

### A Clever Note on Hydration

Water passes through your system quite quickly. If you put glucose into your water, one glucose molecule will attach itself to a couple of water molecules. When you drink this, your body treats it differently to plain water. Your body notices the glucose and thinks it is food. Instead of passing it straight through your system it takes it into your body to process it. As a result, you hydrate your body. Magic!

If you add a drop of fruit juice to your water, the glucose in fruit juice makes this process happen. When you drink pure water, you will notice you will want to go to the toilet to pass it through. However, when you are hydrating yourself, with the glucose/water mix, you will find that you need to go to the toilet much less. Isotonics are a great tool when you are engaging in long distance or time related events.

Only use isotonics when the session is longer than 1 hour, the match or race is longer than 90 minutes and/or if a pre exercise meal isn't possible.

### Protein Supplements

I am often asked about protein supplements – should I or shouldn't I use them.

Protein supplements are commonly used to help increase protein levels and to help build muscle. Many bodybuilders and people interested in building muscle supplement their diet with protein powders. Most protein supplements have artificial sugars and sweeteners, such as Maltodextrin and other products that are associated with causing cancer. They use an artificial protein in the powders which are chemical based. They are not natural and I would suggest that you try to get extra protein from your diet instead of using supplements.

Neil was a client who was training in mixed martial arts and would weight train most days. He complained of headaches frequently. He had used protein supplements for around 15 years, mainly through protein shakes and bars. During our sessions he decided he would cut out protein supplements completely and decided to eat more protein in his diet instead. He concentrated on the lean, clean proteins, such as fish and chicken, and introduced beans into his diet. He quickly found that his headaches disappeared, he had more energy, felt healthier and his head was less muggy.

If you do choose to use protein supplements, they should be an added extra in your diet and not used as a substitute.

**Glycogen or Fat?**
I am often asked what store of energy we use when we exercise. Here is a little information on what you use and when.

Glycogen is the source of energy most used for exercise. It is needed for any short, intense bursts of exercise because it is immediately accessible. Glycogen also supplies energy during the first few minutes of any sport or exercise. During long, slow durations of exercise, fat can help fuel the activity. Glycogen is still needed though to help break down the fat into something the muscles can use.

The type of activity and workout you engage in, will affect the stores of energy you use in your body.

Lower intensity workouts will burn fat and glycogen together. A greater percentage of fat will be taken from the fat stores and used for energy with some glycogen taken from the liver and muscles. Fat takes a while to get converted back to glucose so is used more within lower intensity workouts. Therefore, if you are engaging in low intensity sports, you will need to eat more fat in your diet.

With higher intensity workouts the emphasise shifts towards more glycogen being used and less fat burning. Therefore, if you are engaging in higher intensity sports you will need to introduce more carbohydrates in to your diet.

If you are interval training, you are effectively engaging in a high intensity workout. Therefore, you will need more carbohydrates in your diet.

Marathon runners and those in training: when you run for under 90 minutes, most of your energy comes from stored muscle glycogen. If you're running for longer than 90 minutes, the liver glycogen and sugar in your blood become more important. This is because your muscle glycogen store gets depleted. Fuelling with carbohydrates during your marathon will prevent you from running out of energy and hitting the wall, while also boosting your performance. As you increase your training levels, gradually start to increase the carbohydrate intake so your body gets used to holding on to more glycogen. For optimum performance, make sure you increase your carbohydrate intake on the lead up to the marathon and learn how to refuel with carbohydrates as you run.

Whatever activity or sport you are engaging in, it is important to consider the five stages: fuel up, in activity, top up, mend and recover. If you get your eating right here you will gain optimum performance, you will ensure your recovery is quick and you will make sure your body doesn't get damaged in the process.

Be aware of the activity and exercise you do and think about whether you need to tweak a few things. Do you eat well for the exercise you are engaging in? If not, what do you need to change?

# Chapter 16: Exercise

# Frequently Asked Questions

*There is a lot of competing advice on how much exercise and how often. Recently there was a TV programme stating that 3 minutes of really intense exercise had more health benefits than an hour in the gym. Sometimes it's hard to know what to do for the best, especially when really busy. What do you recommend?*

I think the 3-minute exercise regime is society's way of responding to the fast paced life that we are used to. We want quick, easy fixes. Research is going into whether 3 minutes of very high intensity exercise can give you the same health benefits as an hour in the gym. There will be many other tests and research going on that we aren't aware of.

My personal feeling is that if you engage in very high intensity exercise, it will put a strain on your heart. If you are not used to it, this could cause illness or issues further down the line. I have tried the 3-minute exercise. It hurt my chest so much that I decided not to do it again. Instead, I respond to what feels good when I am doing it. I would recommend listening to your body and trying to be more active every day. Try to fit activity into your daily life. You will see health benefits from this.

### What time of day is best for exercise?

I would suggest that morning is the optimum time for exercise. The reason being, your body and mind will feel the benefits of the exercise all day. Your body can repair and construct and you can refuel throughout the day. That being said, it is very hard for the majority of people to exercise in the morning! I would suggest staying away from late night exercising – your body will be working overtime while you sleep to repair and you may have disrupted sleep as a result. I would also say that any exercise/activity is better than none. So try to be active whenever you can during the day.

### How do you juggle eating around exercising later in the evening?

Make sure you eat healthily before the exercise (so maybe even have your evening meal or if not a snack). Wait for at least 1-2 hours after and then exercise. When you have finished exercising, have a snack to top up your protein and carbohydrate levels. Try not to go straight to bed. Leave 30 minutes to an hour before you do. When you wake in the morning, make sure you get protein and unrefined complex carbohydrates (oats etc.) into your breakfast. This will give you energy but also continue to repair and build muscle.

### Does one size fit all in terms of what should be eaten and the time before/after exercise?

Simple answer here is no. Every person is different and different activities need different fuel (as mentioned in the previous section). Timings are dependent on the activity. For example, I can eat a snack 10 minutes before cycling but I get a stitch if I eat 3 hours before running. Best thing to do with timings is experiment with the activity. Try to keep the activity to the same time of day so you can get a good feel for what will work. Keep your routine and foods the same, just play with the timings.

## Quiz - How Active Are You?

Try out this quiz to see how active you are. Be honest and go with your gut instinct.

**On average, how many days per week do you do at least 30 minutes of physical activity over the day?**
a.  0 - 1
b.  5 or more
c.  2 - 4

**Do you tend to use the:**
a.  Escalator
b.  Stairs
c.  Escalator but keep walking

**In a typical working day, do you:**
a.  Spend most of your time sitting
b.  Spend most of your day standing/moving around
c.  Sit for most of the day but get up frequently

**If you worked in an office and had to talk to someone on the next floor, would you:**
a.  Email or call them
b.  Walk up to see them using the stairs
c.  Walk to see them but take the lift

**I like to:**
a.  Watch my favourite TV programmes, read, watch DVDs and go out for food
b.  Walk, cycle and play tennis. I like to be outdoors
c.  Play golf, but we usually have a cart

**If someone suggested that I lift weights, I would:**
a.  Guffaw. Dumbbells and me? No thanks
b.  Say that I already do. Two or three days a week
c.  Be interested. I know I should, I just don't know how

**When you reach to your toes, you can:**

a.   Are you joking? I can barely see them, never mind reach them!
b.   Reach your shoelaces. Sometimes I can touch the floor
c.   Reach your ankles, but I am definitely not as supple as I used to be!

**My general attitude about exercise is:**

a.   Urgggghhhh. It reminds me of PE
b.   I look forward to it
c.   I know I should but I don't prioritise it in my day

**Now, total up how many a's, b's and c's you have.**

**A = you are not active enough.** You are at risk of health issues if you do not start to be more active. The good news is exercise doesn't have to be painful, boring or time consuming. Just a few minutes every day can dramatically improve your health, outlook and wellbeing. What enjoyable activity could you do to get you up and moving around more?

**B = you are very active.** This is great for your health and wellbeing. By being active every day you are looking after yourself well. Keep up the good work.

**C = the thought is there!** Maybe some motivation and accountability would help? Contact a friend and ask them to help you to become more active. You will see the health benefits straight away if you start to introduce something into every day. Why wait?

## Summary

We have taken a look at exercise and activity. We have looked at the basics and how you can start to build more activity into your day. Take a look at the tips and the summaries and think about how you can tweak a few things in your life right now to give you the time and flexibility to be more active.

If you aren't very active now, I urge you to identify things that you like to do. Then look at how you can build them into your life every day. If you are already active, think about how you can make sure you keep variety in your exercise to spice things up.

We have also taken a look at sports nutrition, for those of you that engage in exercise regularly. This will help you to take your exercise to the next level.

Below are the key things you need to remember and the 8 questions we explored in the section.

**Things to Remember**
- Being active is fundamental to achieving good health and wellbeing.
- Think of getting active as a way to look after your health and wellbeing.
- There are many barriers that you can use to excuse not exercising.
- Having the right attitude to exercise is the key to integrating it into your daily life.
- If you are in pain or feel unwell, stop.
- Regular exercise is the key. Do something every day for at least 20 minutes. You can split this into more manageable chunks.
- Exercise doesn't need to be vigorous.

- You can find ways to fit being active into your daily routine.
- HIIT will help you to lose weight.
- Engage in cardio, strength training and flexibility exercises.
- You don't need to join a gym to be active!
- Be aware of the 5 common misconceptions.

**Sports Nutrition**
- There are 5 stages to eating well around fitness. These are the Fuel Up, In-Activity, Top Up, Mend and Recover stages. Make sure you eat well around all these stages.
- To refuel during the exercise, use natural isotonic drinks.
- Try to eat good quality proteins in your diet instead of taking protein supplements.
- Think about the type of exercise you are doing and the duration and take note on what foods you should be focusing on.
- If you are training for an event, experiment with eating times to get a feel for what will work for you on the day.

**Aspects and Questions to Explore**
- What are your barriers to exercising?
- Set yourself some goals.
- Track your activity.
- What do you do now? Could you do more? What could you do to build more activity into your life?
- Who could you engage with to make it more fun and enjoyable?
- What times of day are you inactive? How could you be more active at these times?
- Do you eat well around the exercise you do?
- What do you need to tweak in your diet to make sure you are fuelling up, topping up, mending and recovering well?

# Part 3:

# Everything You Need to Know About Stress

# Chapter 17: Introduction to Stress

We hear the phrase 'I'm stressed' all the time in the Western World. But do we know what stress actually is and what it means?

The word 'stress' has many negative associations attached to it. If you ask someone if they are stressed, the natural response is a clear and clipped 'no' followed by defensive body language. More frequently people are becoming ill and developing all sorts of pains and ailments associated with stress.

Let us look in this section at stress in more detail. We will look at what stress is, how your body reacts to stressful situations and the consequences on your health. We will then look at practical things you can do to reduce and manage your stress levels. And to finish off, a little quiz.

**What is Stress?**
Stress is the body's way of responding to any kind of demand. This could be a physical demand, an emotional demand, a mental demand or a demand to change. Stress is something that creates a sense of threat, usually by confronting a person with a demand for something or an opportunity for change.

We all react very differently to stressful events and situations and as a result, we all have different ways that stress affects the body. Do you know how your body reacts to stressful situations? If not, don't worry. We will be looking at this in more detail and you will have the opportunity to identify how you react to stressful situations.

When I am stressed, I feel shaky, tense and get a dry mouth. My friend loses weight, gets a lot of headaches and is very irritable. Everyone has a different response to stress and experience different feelings, thoughts, actions, and bodily responses. We will look at these a little later on.

Stress can be caused by both good and bad experiences. Most people associate stress with the bad experiences and overlook the stress caused by the good experiences. It still exists, even though it is good!

Stress is a very normal physical response to events that make you feel threatened, frightened or upset your balance in some way. Many people think stress is an unnatural thing and that you should avoid it at all costs. In the modern, fast paced and technological world, this isn't possible.

Did you know that 1 in 6 people are experiencing stress in Britain? Or that 1 in 2 of us will be stressed at some stage? Stress is more common than you think.

# Chapter 18: Caveman Dave

When you sense danger (whether this danger is real or imagined) the body's defences go into what is commonly known as the 'fight or flight' reaction, or the stress response. I name the person that we all become **'Caveman Dave'**. We all have Caveman Dave within us.

'Fight or flight' is the body's way of protecting you and helps you rise to meet the challenges ahead. It is triggered by a sense of threat. It is a primitive survival instinct and was designed to protect us and make sure we don't die.

Think back to the day of the caveman. Imagine this scene for me, if you will. A caveman is out collecting wood to build a fire. He is very cold and tired and needs some warmth after a busy day hunting. As he is scouring around the floor and picking up all of his finds, a sabre-tooth tiger in the distance spots the caveman. The tiger is out hunting and at the sight of the caveman, his mouth begins to water. The tiger races through the undergrowth to reach the caveman. The caveman hears the tiger as he races towards him and is very scared. He drops all the logs he has been gathering and all of a sudden he can move a lot faster, jump a lot higher and think faster.

The caveman's 'fight or flight' response kicked in as soon as he saw the tiger. He was faced with two options. Do I fight or do I run away? Which would you have done?

## Processes Taking Place

So what happened within the caveman's body at that moment when he saw the tiger? Simply, when you feel stressed by something going on around you, your body reacts by releasing chemicals into the blood. These chemicals give you more energy and strength, which is a good thing if your stress is caused by physical danger, such as being faced with the sabre-tooth tiger.

The 'fight or flight' response is initiated in a part of the brain called the hypothalamus. The hypothalamus sets up a sequence of chemical relays to the pituitary glands and then on to the adrenal glands. This causes a number of stress hormones to be released into the blood stream. As a result, the body responds in a variety of ways. The caveman's body reacted in this instance to help him to survive the danger.

In the moment, the caveman will have experienced mental and physical reactions. I detail what these may have been below.

**Mental Reactions**
- Increased focus, concentration and alertness
- Increased mental activity for thinking about the situation
- Heightened awareness of everything around him

**Physical Reactions**
- Increased heart rate and blood pressure
- Increased breathing rate
- Increased muscle contraction
- Pupil dilation of the eyes for clear vision
- Increased blood sugar (needed for strength and endurance)
- Increased blood clotting to minimize injury
- Increased blood to muscles
- Decreased perception of pain (until the danger disappears)
- Decreased blood flow to the logical and rational parts of the brain (we don't need these in the moment)

Any bodily functions not needed to help in this instance are shut down. Digestion stops, blood flow to internal organs decreases and the immune system is suppressed to conserve energy. When our physical survival is threatened, the fight or flight response is fantastic. Our bodies are very clever!

However, it can also be a bad thing when our bodies don't just use it for a short-term survival mechanism, as it was intended to be used.

These days, we very rarely shut off the Caveman Dave response. Instead of the sabre-tooth being our threat, we have replaced him with missing deadlines, paying the bills on time and dealing with the morning rush hour traffic. We see EVERYTHING as a threat and move into the attack position with our nearest and dearest, within our jobs and even strangers on the street.

Other common causes of stress are: the death of a loved one, divorce and separation, money problems, relationship issues, exam stress and learning, family problems, work worries, bullying and changes in your home circumstances – such as moving out or your children leaving. These are all upsetting and will cause the stress response to kick in. How long this lasts is like the saying, how long is a piece of string.

If your stress is in response to something other than the physical threats (such as dealing with a fire, saving someone in an accident or a threat to your life) you will find there is no outlet for this extra energy and strength brought on by Caveman Dave. It will all sit within you. You will feel the responses to the stress but unless you do something about the situation, you will store this extra energy and strength inside.

Beyond a certain point, stress stops being helpful and starts causing major damage to your health, your mood, your productivity, your relationships and your quality of life.

**Stress Related Illnesses**

Stress causes damage to your health when it is experienced frequently. Just think, if your body is in Caveman Dave mode all the time, it is not relaxed and at ease. When you are 'at the top of the tree' (as my mum calls it) all the time, you can only expect to see health issues.

It is believed there is a direct connection between the body's reaction to stress and its negative effects on our physical health.

Here are a few of the main stress related disorders.
- Heart disease
- High blood pressure
- Immune system disorders
- Migraine headaches
- Sleep disturbances
- Sexual dysfunction
- Diabetes
- Stroke
- Cancer
- Pituitary disorder
- Adrenal exhaustion

Many people complain of aches and pains in their bodies. If there hasn't been any kind of trauma to these areas, they are caused by stress. If you are stressed and you aren't releasing the energy somewhere, it builds up inside until it manifests as aches and pains. I will discuss ways to release this energy later on in this section.

Not only does it have physical effects, it also has effects on our mental health, emotional health and spiritual health.

If you learn to manage stress, this will help to reduce aches, pains and anxiety levels. You are also more likely to take care of yourself and be motivated to seek a more fulfilling life.

**Your Response**
Stress can affect your feelings, thoughts, actions and your body. Let us take a look at the common responses you will see as a result of stress.

When you are stressed, you may feel any of the following: uptight, flat, self-conscious, at the end of your tether, cut off from others, easily upset and feel guilty easily. You may be embarrassed easily, feel low a lot of the time, full of anger, get jealous quickly, feel discomfort easily and insecure. You may also have lost your sense of humour, feel without hope, tearful and that stress brings out the worst in you.

When you are stressed, this affects your thoughts, be it consciously or not. You may notice that you worry over things you know you shouldn't worry about, lose your self-confidence, think your memory is poor, find it hard to concentrate, find it hard to relax your mind and think that you can't control your world. You may have lost interest in a lot of things, are easily startled, may not like yourself, may be waiting for the worst to happen, are easily confused and think you have no get up and go.

You may avoid doing things or going places as you feel you will not be able to cope with them, you may be more quick tempered or angry, withdrawing from life. You may be unable to sit at peace, be making more mistakes, try to 'play safe' more than usual and avoid responsibility. You may also be drinking more than you should, smoking more, eating a lot more or a lot less, be more tearful and let others walk over you more often.

Your body will be affected by stress. You may have a lot of aches and pains due to tense muscles, be more prone to colds and flu, feel drained of energy and never feel 100%. You may lose or gain weight, get a lot of headaches, feel your breathing changes when tense and feel you have to push yourself through the day. Your body may feel uptight much of the day and you may find that your body reacts very easily to stress. You may even find it hard to get to sleep or stay asleep. Some people find they need to go to the toilet more frequently (either to urinate or to empty their bowels).

It is important to realise that not everyone who feels stressed will feel, think, act or have the same bodily responses. Each person reacts differently to stress and will experience different things.

Take a moment now to think about how stress affects you. If you are struggling, think about the last situation you were in when you know you were definitely stressed. Try to remember how you felt, what thoughts were going through your head, how you acted and what was going on in your body. Make a note of all the things that you experienced on this occasion. This will help you to identify what goes on for you when you are stressed.

It will also help you to notice when you are in a stressful situation. Sometimes stressful events and situations creep up on you and before you know it you are in the thick of it. Knowing how you react to stress can help you to realise when one of these instances has crept up on you. Once you are aware of the situation, you can then start to manage the situation and your stress levels appropriately.

# Chapter 19: Managing Stress

In this chapter, I will outline my top tips on how to manage your stress levels and to take back control of the Caveman Dave response. The aim here is to minimise the amount of time you spend being a caveman and spend more time being the lovely you.

I have split the chapter into three parts. The first details how to look after your body. The second details how to look after your mind and the third details how to look after your spirit.

### Are There Any Hidden Problems?

First of all, let us check something fundamental. You must check that your stress isn't trying to tell you there is something wrong in your life. Are there any problems you need to face up to? Are you burying your head a little in the sand, knowing deep down, that you feel this way because there is something you are trying to suppress and hide away from?

For example, this may be issues within a certain relationship (plutonic or sexual) or an issue surrounding a child, friend or parent. It could be issues related to money, work or addictions such as gambling, drink or drugs. It may even be issues surrounding maturity, stubbornness or dependency on people/situations.

If you don't acknowledge hidden problems, this can add to the stress and you will find that you struggle to control it. You will also find that the stress lies underlying for a long time, until you deal with the situation.

Ok, so let us now look at some ideas, tips and tools to help you when you are feeling stressed. Try these out, explore them and see what works for you. I have split the ideas into different sections, for ease.

##  Looking After Your Body

**Exercise regularly.**
There are many health benefits to exercise, such as it helps to manage a healthy weight, reduces blood pressure, keeps bones, muscles and joints healthy, improves your body shape and extends life. It also reduces the risk of heart disease, diabetes, some cancers and Alzheimer's. Serotonin (a chemical in the brain to control the mood) is low in people who suffer from anxiety. Exercise releases serotonin. This will raise the mood and help you to feel better.

Exercise is not only good for physical health and has psychological benefits but also gives time and space away from the situation.

Engage in moderate rather than hard exercise; enough to raise your heart rate but so you are still able to hold a conversation with someone.

Why not try out activities such as lifting weights, dancing, jogging, running, swimming, cycling, golf, football, badminton, a brisk walk or an aerobics video/class. Make it more fun by engaging the whole family!
Eat a balanced diet. We have already looked at this in a lot of detail so no further comment!

**Sleep well.**
Make sure you get enough sleep. This will help to keep your concentration and help deal and respond appropriately to pressure.

I am often asked about sleep and how to get the best out of it. Here are a few ideas:

**Your bedroom:** make sure the bed and room are warm. Is your bed comfy or old and in need of replacing? Are your pillows comfy? Are the curtains keeping out the light? If not, buy new ones. Make it as comfortable as you can.

**Noise:** control as much noise inside the house as you can. Turn the heating off, electrical appliances and shut out the dog/cat. Do what you can to minimise the noises in your house, including buzzing of electric appliances. You can't stop external noises but can manage the internal noises.

**Your partner:** if your partner snores or is restless, ask if he or she can move to another room. They must move, not you. You need to learn to sleep well in your own bed. Do this nicely... Once you are able to sleep well in your own bed reintroduce your partner!

**Exercise:** can help you sleep better. Do this in the morning, afternoon or early evening. Don't do it 3 hours before bedtime.

**Relax before bed:** try to slow down for the hour before bed. Listen to music, read a book, have a bath. If you work late shifts or are studying late, don't go straight to bed from your work. Give yourself time to switch off.

**Caffeine:** is a stimulant. Try to cut down your caffeine intake across the day. Try to avoid drinking it from late afternoon onwards. The effects of too much caffeine can be very similar to those of stress. It increases the heart rate and makes you feel hot and sweaty.

**Smoking:** nicotine is also a stimulant. Avoid smoking in the 3 hours before bedtime. Never smoke during the night if you wake up.

**Alcohol:** if you drink, as the alcohol level in your blood drops, it will wake you up. This usually happens after 2-4 hours. It will be hard to get back off to sleep. It disrupts your sleep rhythms and cuts down the rapid eye movement and deep sleep. You won't feel properly rested. Alcohol will also exacerbate the issues surrounding the stress. Initially it can help you to relax. It can cause issues of its own though – arguments or heightened feelings and poor sleep. You will feel groggy in the morning and this will impact on your thoughts, feelings and physically throughout the next few days.

**Food:** try not to eat for around 2 hours before you go to bed. Your body will start to work to digest the food. If you are hungry, take a light snack one hour before sleep. Try not to eat during the night if you wake up.

**Drink:** try to drink as little as possible in the evening. This may stop you waking to use the toilet in the night.

**Your sleeping needs:** most of us sleep for around 7-8 hours per night. You need less sleep as you get older. The amount of sleep you need depends on your lifestyle. If you are busy and on the go, you may need more sleep. If you are not active during the day, you may need less. You need to find your own optimum level.

**Learn to relax.**
Try meditation, visualisations, deep breathing exercises, reading a book or listening to music. Find what works for you and do this every day.

Here is one relaxation technique that helps to release tension. Start off by tensing each muscle in turn in your body and then release the tension. Start at your head and work down your body. Do this all the way over the body so you know what each body part feels like to be tense and what relaxed feels like.

**Practical Things You Can Do**

Take things one step at a time. Don't try to do everything all at once. Be clear about what you need to do and plan ahead so you can achieve it.

Achieve something, however small. This can help lift the spirit and mood.

Don't avoid the situation that is making you feel stressed. It will just make it worse. Try to tackle it. If you need help, ask for it.

Learn to say no. You don't have to do everything.

Be better organised and don't leave things until the last minute.

Do you have a problem or an issue you are trying to deal with? Here is one way I have found works for me to break through it.

Firstly, state clearly what the problem or issue is. Grab a piece of paper and a pen for this one. Write down your problem or issue. Think about what will happen if you don't solve this problem. Brainstorm solutions, either alone or with a friend. Bouncing ideas off others helps to generate fresh ideas you may not have thought of alone. Once you have a list of ideas, choose the best option. Write the pros and cons of each idea to help you decide. When you have your idea(s) to take the issue forward, work out a plan on how you will do these things. Then put it into action. If you need others to help, ask them and share with them what you are trying to achieve. People want to help others. Sometimes, you just need to ask. When you have put the plan into action, review it. Did it work? If not, why not? What did you learn? Can you improve anything to make it better?

Do you have a fear of something? Use the same method as above with your fear in mind. Seriously, this method is great and works really well if you work with someone else.

## ♥ Looking After Your Mind

Write a list of everything you are good at. Do this when you are sat alone and have a few minutes peace. Write the list and include all the things you know you are good at, the things people tell you that you are good at and the things you enjoy doing. Keep it to hand and look at it when you have a wobble, need a boost or need to put things into perspective.

Be kind to yourself and learn from your mistakes. Don't use them to hit yourself over the head with daily. We are our own worst critics. Try to be as kind to you as you are to your friends. Look at a situation, learn from it and apply the learning the next time round. Don't keep thinking about the past and things that haven't gone well or right for you. Focus on making the next time better and positive.

Talk to someone you trust about the situation that you are in. Talking it through can help it feel more manageable and help you to find a different perspective on the situation. It is useful to talk it through so you can find solutions and look at options for dealing with it. Talking out loud helps to generate new thoughts and ideas.

If you are not feeling well, give yourself time out. Recognise when you need time out and take it. Even if this is in the middle of an important meeting or where you are expected to deliver something.

When I recognise the stress kicking in, I make an excuse to stand up and change my physiology. Moving breaks the thoughts and feelings that are going on inside me and make me focus on something else for a moment.

If you feel the need to leave the room for a moment, so you can take a breather and get some air, say you need to use the toilet or that you need a drink or something to eat. This can

170

give you the time away to get your head back in the right space and to give you a moment to compose and refocus. Don't be afraid to do this. When I have said this to people, they worry about what others will think of them. In reality, they will think you needed the toilet, a drink or something to eat. They do not know what is going on within your head or your body.

## What About Your Thoughts?

Stress feeds our negative thoughts. Having negative thoughts feeds the stress some more. To break this negative cycle you need to change your thoughts. Here are a few ideas of how to do this:

To put things into perspective when you are dwelling on an issue, ask yourself one of these 5 questions.

1. What are the chances of X happening?
2. What is the worst thing that could happen?
3. Am I right to think X?
4. What is this worth?
5. Will this really matter in 5 years?

Ask yourself the question and challenge the negative thoughts you are having. Think about where this thought has come from, answer the question and then think it through. Does this really matter to you? Find evidence to get rid of the thought. Doing this will help you to put the issue into perspective.

If you have a stressful situation coming up, try this. A technique I like to call 'Bashing Through'.

Firstly, identify any situations you know that you find stressful. It may be general situations or you may have something coming up that you know will be difficult. This could be delivering a presentation to a room full of people or something as simple as getting on a bus alone.

Then think about preparing for it. So think about what you could do to make it less stressful. The bus scenario – you might want to research the bus times, think about how long it takes to get to the bus stop, try out the timings, look at the number of stops before the one you are getting off at. You may even want to do the route with a friend a few times so you are used to the route. Do whatever you can beforehand to take the stress out of the occasion.

Then go through with it. Remember to keep thinking and don't jump to any conclusions. If there are any things you prepared for use on the day, keep these in mind and live in the moment. Don't worry about the past or what may happen in the future. Keep your eye and your mind on the here and now. Expect there to be stress but know you are living with it and getting through the experience in a positive way.

After the event, review how it all went. How did you do? Was the event as stressful as you anticipated? What could you do better next time around? Make a note of these things and keep practicing whenever you can.

It is very important that you don't avoid the situation. Short term this may help the situation but longer term, this will cause major problems for you. Bash through these stressful situations and know at the other side, you will be healthy, happy and stress free.

## ♥ Looking After Your Spirit

Do something that makes you happy or have fun. Remember back to when you were a child. What did you like to do? What gave you joy and made you excited? For some it would be hopscotch and others it might be water fights, building dens or camping in the field or garden. Why not do these now?

**Indulge** in a pleasure giving activity without feeling any guilt. If you feel guilt, there is no point in taking part in the activity. Make the decision to do something and enjoy it.

**Engage** in a social activity with other people. This reminds us that we can enjoy ourselves and are social beings.

Get outside into **nature** whenever you can. This will refresh your body, mind and spirit.

Spend more time with people who have a good, light **energy** about them. Restrict time with negative and draining people. Surround yourself with these positive and upbeat people.

**Notice** what you have achieved and think about the positive things that have happened in your day/week. Take time to reflect on all the things you do well.

**Mantras.** These help to keep your mind occupied and focused on a certain thing. Try repeating a positive statement to yourself a few times. For example, I am in control or I am calm. This will help you to refocus and think about something else for a few minutes so you can put everything into perspective.

**Breathing.** Sit, close your eyes and simply focus on your breathing. Notice how it feels as you breathe in and out. Slow your breathing right down and simply focus on your breath.

This will help to calm you down and reground you. It also has massive health benefits.

**Meditation.** I will talk about this in more detail in the next section. Meditation is a valuable tool to help you to manage your stress levels and is well documented for its health benefits. This is an extremely beneficial way to relax, which is commonly used when working with spirit and with those wanting spiritual awakening and growth.

If you need to take time out for a moment and to distract yourself, try to describe what you see. Describe something you can see in great detail.

**Worry time.** Set aside 15 minutes in the evening to worry about the things that have bothered you throughout the day. If you start to worry in the morning, stop and store it for later. At the start of your worry time, you must think of all the things you set aside to worry about. Chances are you won't be able to remember them.

## Over to You

So, I have outlined a variety of tools and ideas that will help you to look after your body, mind and spirit. Hopefully, this has given you something to think about and lots of different things you can try out.

I want you to take a moment now to think about these two questions.

What are the key things coming to mind here that you need to think more about?

What do you want to try out to help to deal with stressful situations?

Remember, there are no miracle cures for stress. You need to practise all of these things on a regular basis to gain benefits and to lead a more relaxed and carefree life.

## Quiz - How Stressed Are You?

Try out this quiz to see how stressed you are. Be honest and go with your gut instinct.

**Answer yes or no to the following questions:**

1. Do you eat badly, quickly and grab on the go?
2. Do you try to do everything yourself and don't say no to anyone or anything?
3. Do you get angry quickly or are you easily irritated?
4. Do you fail to see the humour in situations that others find funny?
5. Do you keep everything bottled up inside?
6. Do you get limited exercise and fresh air?
7. Do you have limited supportive relationships?
8. Do you get too little rest and sleep?
9. Do you frequently put things off until later?
10. Do you think there is only one right way to do something?
11. Do you neglect to relax every day or take time out?
12. Do you spend a lot of time complaining about the past?
13. Do you race through the day thinking of the future?
14. Do you feel unable to cope with all you have to do?
15. Do you worry about situations when you are in bed?
16. Do you lack fun and happiness in your life at the moment?

**If you answered mainly yes**, you are showing distinct signs of stress. It is time to take a step back and to think about your lifestyle, career and relationships. Slow down and think about what is going on for you right now. What is causing you stress at the moment? How can you minimise the stress in your life so you are not showing signs of Caveman Dave on a regular basis? What can you do to slow down and have more fun in your life? Make this a priority before your health makes the decision for you.

**If you answered mainly no,** you are showing that stress isn't a big part of your life at the moment. Keep applying the strategies you are using now and look after yourself. Maybe try out some new strategies to spice things up a little. Keep up the good work.

## Summary

Having looked at stress; what it is, how your body reacts to stressful situations and the consequences on your health, you should have a better idea of what stress looks and feels like for you. You may feel that stress doesn't affect you. I encourage you to think about your life and where there are areas of tension at the moment. You may not feel that stress is in your life. Consciously, it may not be. Subconsciously, it could be.

There were many practical things in this section that you can do to reduce and manage your stress levels and I hope you found something within this that you can try out.

## Summary of Tools and Tips

Here is a reminder of all the tools and tips for reducing stress in your life.

**For the Body**
Exercise
Eat well
Sleep well
Learn to relax
Problem solving method
Face the fear

**For the Mind**
What are you good at?
Be kind to yourself
Talk to someone
Take time out
Challenge your thoughts
Bashing through

**For the Spirit**
Have fun
Be social with positive people
Get outside
Look at what you have achieved
Mantras
Breathing
Meditation
Describe what you see
Worry time

## Questions to Explore

- How does stress affect your body, thoughts, feelings and actions?
- How do you know when you are in a stressful situation?
- What are the key things coming to mind here that you need to think more about?
- What do you want to try out to help to deal with stressful situations?

# Part 4:
# Everything You Need to Know About Living in Spirit

# Chapter 20: Importance of Spirit

**The spirit.** A part of our being that is vastly overlooked. Life happens and we find the time (only just, maybe) to eat, drink and sleep. With all the hustle and bustle of life, work, commitments, responsibilities, family and friends, it is becoming increasingly more difficult to find time for you.

Can you honestly say that you look after yourself and do things just for you every single day? Most people can't and don't.

When events in your life slow down or are a little less manic, you will notice a difference in your thinking, your behaviour and your relationships with those all around you. I certainly notice a change for the better in me.

Wouldn't it be fantastic to be in this slower and more meaningful time more often? I call this time 'living in spirit'.

In this section I will show you how you can live in spirit more frequently. I will introduce you to a number of thoughts, ideas and tools that can have a massive impact on your health, wellbeing and spiritual growth. I have chosen to introduce you to these because I use these strategies on a daily basis and have noticed a vast improvement to many areas of my life as a result. I want you to experience this for yourself. For instance, I am feeling healthier than I have ever felt, I feel physically fit and strong, I experience joy and light in each and every day and I have great, loving relationships with all those that I surround myself with.

I ask that you read this section with an open mind and think about how you can try out these ideas for yourself. When you build these strategies and ideas into your daily life, you will see the benefits. If you do these things once every month (or even once a year!), you are less likely to see the full benefits that these can give you. Make sure you prioritise these strategies and do them every day.

So let's get started.

# Chapter 21: How to Nurture Yourself

Who do you look after the most? When I ask my clients that question, the usual response I get is either 'my kids, my husband, my wife or my parents/grandparents'. It is very rare that people say 'me.'

Why is that? Why do people give everything they have to look after those that are close to them and fail to notice themselves? It is a very common occurrence. When you hear the term 'self-love' do you think of this as a negative thing and something that is frowned upon? Where has all this negativity come from around 'self-love'? How do you feel when you hear the word 'self-love'?

I like to think of it in this way. If you don't look after you, no-one else will. You are the only one that can truly nurture yourself and give your body, mind and spirit what it needs to live, flourish and be fully alive in every given moment.

So why wouldn't you start to prioritise you? I am not saying that you should forget everyone else and only concentrate on you. What I am saying is that, without giving yourself what you need first and foremost, you are less likely to care for others in the best possible way you can. If you are ill and you ignore it, you won't be able to offer the great care and love that is within you to others. Focus on your health and wellbeing and then care for others. You will be more effective this way.

So how can you start to look after yourself more? Here are six key things to think about.

**Water.** Make sure you drink plenty of fresh, clear water on a daily basis. As explored earlier on, this has massive health benefits and ensures you are in peak physical health.

**Good quality, healthy foods.** Make sure the foods you eat nourish you and support your healthy, balanced lifestyle. Cut out all the crap and eat the best foods that you can. If something makes you feel unwell, sluggish or less than 100%, cut it out in future.

**Take time out.** This will help you to put things into perspective and give you space to reflect on everything going on in your life at the moment. If you don't take time out, you will feel fraught, mentally exhausted and may hit burnout much sooner than you thought was possible. Try to take time out every day and do something fun, exciting or that you enjoy. Alternatively, just sit and get quiet. This will give your mind the time to be still and at peace.

**Relaxation.** Build time into every day to relax. This might involve taking a bath, reading a book or listening to music. It might involve having a holistic treatment or curling up on the sofa with a family pet. Whatever relaxation looks like for you, try to give yourself some time every day to do it. It will help you to feel at peace, more grounded and help to manage the stress within your life. I will talk about relaxation in more detail later on.

**Sleep.** Make sure you get plenty of sleep. It is fundamental to recovery and good mental health. It will help you to recharge your batteries and rest your body and mind. Find your optimum level and make sure you get this every night.

**Keep active.** You will notice differences to your energy levels, your health and your wellbeing if you keep active every day. I don't necessarily mean you should be exercising heavily every day. By keeping active I mean keep moving. This will help to keep things moving around your body as they should.

You may notice if you don't move much, that you feel sluggish and tired quite a lot. Start moving a little more and this will change.

## Over to You

Think about these 6 key things for a moment. Do you prioritise these 6 things in your life right now? If not, which ones are lacking in your life and stood out for you as you read them? Make a note of these. Have a think about what you could do to prioritise those that are lacking. What could you do and how will you do that on a daily basis? What do you need to tweak to enable this to happen? Start to prioritise yourself today.

So those are my top 6 tips on how to nurture yourself. Do these on a regular basis and you will start to see differences in all aspects of your life. I found that I became so much more relaxed, which meant that I was being nicer to those around me, I was enjoying the simplest of things much more and I felt at peace. Who wouldn't want that?

# Chapter 22: Law of Attraction

The law of attraction is an ancient principle that originates (I believe) back to Greek philosophy before Socrates. Since this time many philosophers, scientists, writers and even filmmakers have talked about the law of attraction. If you want to read more about the law of attraction, there are many books out there on the subject. One of my favourites is Rhonda Byrne's 'The Secret'. Give it a read.

In essence, the law of attraction states that 'like attracts like'. I tend to think of it as 'what you think about, you bring about'. We all have the ability to bring about everything that we desire, whether we are conscious of this or not. Everything you have experienced in your life to date is a culmination of all the thoughts you have ever had. That is quite a scary prospect but it is reality.

I like to think of it this way. If you think positive things, you will draw positive situations and people to you. However, if you think negative things, you will draw negative situations and people to you.

Now, imagine this situation. You have been asked to go out with your new boyfriend/girlfriend and their friends. You don't know them that well and you don't seem to gel with a few of them, for whatever reason. Your new partner really wants you to go out and to meet them all again. You are not so sure. You think, 'I am going to have a really rubbish night. I am not going to enjoy any moment of it. I am going to be bored and fed up. I really don't like ... and we will spend the night bickering.' The next day, upon reflection, I am certain that all these things were true for you. You did have a rubbish night. You didn't enjoy it. You were bored and fed up and you did spend the night bickering. See how your thoughts became your reality?

Now imagine this situation. You have been asked to go to a family wedding. There will be people there that you haven't seen for such a long time. Family and friends that you have wanted to catch up with for some time but haven't quite got around to it. You are excited and have already got an outfit in mind. You think, 'I am so excited about this. I am really looking forward to seeing …. and catching up with …. I am going to have such a great time. I will spend the night dancing and having fun.' The next day, upon reflection, I am certain you were lying in bed thinking that you had the most amazing time and remembered all the great conversations you had and the laughing that you did throughout the day.

Can you see how the law of attraction works in reality?

The language you choose to speak to yourself with (both internally and externally) and the images you create and hold in your mind have a direct connection to your outward experience. Remember that what you think about you bring about.

Learn to manage your internal expectations and thoughts because reality will meet them. Ditch all the negativity, doubt and fear. After all, do you really want all the negative aspects and your fears to be realised? Only allow yourself to think about the positive things, people and opportunities you want in your life. These will then be drawn in abundance towards you.

Now, just a note here. You can't just sit on the sofa and think 'I want to have a million pounds' and expect it to come through your letter box the very next day. It doesn't work like that.

You need to be clear about what it is you want. Have a desire, a specific goal. Establish your reason for wanting it. Then ask for it. You may want to do this in your mind, out loud, write it down on paper or tell someone about it.

You need to believe that what you have asked for is possible and will come to you. It may not come in the way you expected it or wanted it but believe that it will present itself in one form or another. It may not come in the time frame that you expected either. Be patient.

Action is then needed. What do you need to do to enable it to happen? You might need to change a few things to allow room for the desire to come about. You may need to develop yourself personally or grow a little somewhere in your life to allow what you want to be integrated successfully into your life. You can't just sit back and expect it to land in your lap.

When the time is right and you are in the place and space you need to be (physically, mentally and spiritually), you will receive.

## Over to You

Let us think about the law of attraction now and your life.

What is it that you want in your life? Is there something specific that you are aiming for? It may be in your home life, your career, your relationships, personal development or even related to a hobby. If so, what is it? Write it down.

Think about the reasons for you wanting this. Do you actually want this, or is it someone else's want?

Once you have defined what it is you want, ask for it.

Then have the belief that it will happen. What actions do you need to take, be it physically, mentally or spiritually for these things to come about? How are you going to take these actions and when? Do you need to share this with anyone else? Can anyone you know help you with this? If so, share it!

Look out for all the opportunities and things that come your way to help you to achieve it. Keep your eyes and ears open and acknowledge when things are starting to present themselves for you. Take note, say a little thank you and enjoy the journey.

# Chapter 23: Thinking Positively

Following on from the law of attraction and the principle that 'what you think about, you bring about', I want to talk about positive mental attitude.

Remember that I said if you think positively, it will bring positive opportunities and events into your life. However, if you think negatively you will go on a downward spiral.

Your thoughts are very important. If you have negative thoughts, this will feed negative feelings and behaviours. If you think positive thoughts, it can only produce positive feelings and behaviours. Which would you choose if you had the chance? Well, guess what? You do have the choice. Yes it might mean a bit of change and work on your part, but it is possible.

First of all, let us establish what form your thoughts currently take. Here is an activity for you to try out:

**Negative Thoughts Diary**
Over the next 2 or 3 days, I want you to think about the quality of your thoughts. Are they mainly positive, mainly negative or somewhere in between? Are there any specific areas or situations in your life where you think more negatively than others?

If you find it easier, grab yourself a notepad and write down the thoughts you have throughout the day. Then at the end of the 2 or 3 days, take a look back for any patterns you see.

What do you notice? Are you surprised by anything you see there?

I ask a large proportion of my clients to do this. Charlie always professed that she was a positive thinker. When she looked back at her 3-day diary, she noticed that she was largely a positive thinker. However, when she spent time with a certain person at work, she delved into very negative thinking and gossiping. This was a shock to her and she hadn't been aware of this pattern. She decided she wanted to do something about it.

Since she was aware of the pattern around this person, she was more aware of her thoughts and behaviours when talking to her. Charlie decided she didn't want to gossip about anyone (since it brought her energy down and wasn't a nice thing to do) and when the lady started to gossip about a fellow colleague, she politely said 'I would rather not talk about others while they are not here to respond.' This was very difficult for Charlie to do at first, but she stuck to her word and changed the subject. After just 3 times of saying this over a week, the lady began to take note and stopped gossiping with Charlie.

Charlie also noted her thoughts when she was with this lady. At first, she struggled to do anything about her thoughts. But then, she realised that because she was aware of the negative thoughts, she was more able to do something about it. She decided that as soon as a negative thought came into her head, she would replace it with a positive thought instead. This took quite a bit of retraining but after 3 weeks she was able to control her thoughts. She noticed as a result that her behaviours changed around this lady and she was more positive in interactions with her. She was able to respond to the lady within conversations in a more positive way, which made the lady question her own thoughts too.

Charlie is not the only person to have done this. I have seen a large proportion of my clients take on their thoughts and retrain their minds. Remember, it takes approximately 21 days to change a habit and to form a new one. The key thing here is not to beat yourself up if you miss a negative thought or if you voice negativity. Just realise you have done it and think about how you could notice it next time.

Do you think you could benefit from doing this? If so, get started today. The results will astound you.

Let us now consider thinking positively.

If you adopt a positive outlook in your day you will see improvements in many areas of your life. You will see an improvement in your health, relationships and overall quality of life.

By focusing on the positive aspects of your life, you can reduce your stress (which can lead to a suppressed immune system, heart disease etc.) You will also reduce your anxiety levels and are more likely to take care of yourself and be motivated to seek a more fulfilling life.

You will see an improvement in your personal and professional relationships and overall effectiveness. You will be more motivated to achieve success, meet the goals you have and get help and advice from those around you. When you are happy and optimistic, people enjoy your company. If you are miserable and moaning all the time, people will avoid spending time with you.

Thinking positively takes you away from the negative. You are more likely to think of all the good things you have in your life and of all the things you are thankful for. Then, with the law of attraction in mind, you will attract more of these things. You are more likely to be able to put things into perspective too.

There are many benefits to thinking positively; too many to mention here. I hope this gives you some inspiration to start to think positively about every aspect of your life.

## Over to You

I want you to write a few lists or draw a few pictures for me now. You can use these to get you thinking positively when you are having a lapse. Oh yes, you will have lapses from time to time. After all, you are only human. So grab a piece of paper or a notebook and keep this somewhere you can see it when you are feeling less positive.

- What are your strengths – personal and professional?
- What do you love?
- What is great in your life right now?
- What do you have in abundance in your life?
- What makes you feel truly alive and joyful?

When you are caught in negativity and want to draw yourself out, consider these 2 questions:

1. What are the positives to the situation?
2. What good things have happened in your day?

Focus on the positive as often as you can. You will see massive shifts in how you approach and view life.

# Chapter 24: Affirmations

A great way to think more positively and to attract good things into your life is to use affirmations throughout the day. Affirmations are simple. They are you being in conscious control of your thoughts. They are short, powerful statements that say who you want to be and how you want to experience your life. When you say them, think them or even hear them, they become the thoughts that create your reality. You can program your subconscious mind to create changes and improvements in your life. We can make the decision to change the content of our subconscious mind. It is more powerful than the conscious mind, so start to be in control of it!

Here are a few common affirmations:
- I am a success in all that I do.
- I feel happy, I feel healthy, I feel great.
- Everything feels so right.
- My mind is clear, focused and energised.

## Over to You

Write yourself a few positive affirmations and recite them at least 3 times a day. I tend to recite just as I get up, at lunchtime and before I go to bed. Say them out loud if you can or mentally if you can't.

Be sure to only work with a few affirmations at a time. Don't overwhelm yourself by taking on any more than 2 or 3.

When you say the affirmations, visualise yourself being that person, behaving in that way or doing what it is you are saying. Creating pictures in your mind's eye will help to cement it within your subconscious mind. Try to hear the sounds playing out all around you and feel the emotions that you would feel. Make it as real as you can so it can filter into the subconscious and start to play itself out in reality.

# Chapter 25: How to Live in the Moment

There are three time periods that we can think about. These are the past, the present and the future.

When you think of the past, you probably relive the things that you messed up on. Or maybe you think about how embarrassed you were when you did something. Maybe you wish you could have something back that is gone. Are you living in memories of good times that have past? Or are you angry about things that have been done to you?

When you think of the future, are you worrying about things that need to be done later? Or are you worrying about what might happen tomorrow? Maybe you have concerns over a big event that is coming up. Are you anxious that things might go wrong, or that you might mess something up? Maybe you are hoping for something wonderful and dreaming of great things to come.

When you are in the present you are focused on what you are doing and what is happening right now, at this moment.

If you spend most of your time thinking about the past or future, you are missing life as it happens. It is passing you by while you are elsewhere, be it the past or the future. You will not get the most out of life unless you learn to focus on being present, while things are happening in real time.

Just think for a moment. How often do you hear people talking about how things used to be and dwelling on how things have changed? Or overhear people wishing their life away by saying 'I can't wait for …'? Have you ever overheard people focusing on the now and what is in front of them at that specific moment in time? It is a rare occurrence unfortunately. Frequently, people tend to live in the past or the future. The here and now is often overlooked. But why?

What is so important that happened last week that is so much more important than the moment you are in right now?

Let me tell you about the benefits I find of living in the moment. My focus has improved within situations I am in and I am better able to tune out distractions around me. I am more creative because my mind is at ease and not buzzing around all over the place. I started to see the beauty in everything around me. I notice the wildlife in my surroundings more, I am aware of how the sun streams through the trees and the colours are intensified in nature. I started to appreciate everything around me and experience the fun and joy in simple activities, such as walking through the park in autumn. I am more playful, with family and friends and with myself. I give myself more freedom to do the things that I want to do and find that I am enjoying life much more. My stress levels dipped dramatically and I am able to get things done much more effectively and faster than before. Who would have thought you could get all that from living in the moment? I certainly didn't expect all of that!

You may find you experience different things when you start to live in the moment more often. Make a note of these as they happen, to remind you of why you are doing this and the benefits it brings to you.

So, let's look now at how you can focus on being present in the moment more often. The aim is to learn to focus on the present moment and take your mind out of the past or the future. By all means, think of the past and future when you want to create a better present. Learn from the past and events that have happened and think about how you can plan for the future to make those present moments more satisfying.

## Ideas to Live in the Present

Think about what you are doing at this moment in time. What are you doing? How are you doing it? How does it feel? How does it look? What can you hear around you? Who else is here? Get fully absorbed in the tasks/conversations you are involved in. Tune out all the distractions that are around you.

Focus on what is right in front of you. Or around you. Or on you. Use your senses. Just look at what's in front of you right now. Listen to the sounds around you. Feel the fabric of your clothes and focus on how they feel. You can, for instance, use the summer sun or rain and how it feels on your skin to connect with the present.

Do just one thing at a time. When you eat, just eat. When you are talking to someone, give them your full attention. Let me give you an example that I come across all the time with my clients.

Sarah was always distracted when she was eating, so much so that it started to cause her issues with her health. Here is the advice I gave to her. When you are eating, don't read or think about something else or iron your clothes (especially if you're eating something that might splatter on the clothes). Just eat. Pay attention to what you're eating. Really experience it — the taste, the texture. Do it slowly. It is the same with anything else you are doing: washing dishes, taking a shower, driving, working and playing. Don't do multiple things at once. Just do what you are doing now, and nothing else. Fully engage in the moment and do what you are doing with 100% of your attention.

Another great way to bring you into the moment is to focus on your breath. Sit and be aware of your breath as you breathe in and out. Notice how it feels to breathe in and out. How does your body move as you do this? Where can you feel the air moving? Do you notice any other sensations in or around your body as you just sit and breathe?

Become more aware of your thoughts. You will inevitably think about the past and future. That is ok. Just become aware of those thoughts and let them leave as gently as they arrive. Awareness will bring change.

Be gentle. If you think about the past or future, do not beat yourself up about it! Don't try to force those thoughts out of your head. Just be aware of them, and gently allow them to leave. Then bring yourself back to the present moment and what you are doing.

Put up reminders. A reminder on your fridge or computer desktop or on your wall is a good thing. Or use a reminder service to send you a daily email. Put something in your pocket so when you touch it, it reminds you to come back into the present moment. Do whatever it takes to keep your focus on being present.

Remember that there is no failure. You will slip into thoughts of the past and the future. If you practice you will learn to focus on the present more often than you do now. You cannot fail, even if you stop doing it for a while. Doing it at all is success. Celebrate every little success that you have and really live the moments you have.

If you want to learn how to become present more often, I suggest you read Spencer Johnson's fantastic book 'The Present'. It is a great read and will give you lots more ideas and insight into how to become more present.

# Chapter 26: Give the Gift of Self-Time

Do you give yourself time every day to do the things you love to do? Or want to do? Or make you laugh? Or make you feel loved? Most people don't. However, they do find the time to make meals for the family, iron the clothes, do the washing, feed the cat/kids/rabbit and watch a film. Many of my clients say they don't have time to do the things they want to do. Yet when they think of how they spend their time every day, they can't pinpoint what they did that filled their time.

## Over to You

### How You Spend Your Time

Think of your day yesterday. Write the times down the left hand side of a page – for every hour. In every hour slot, write down what you did. How did you spend that hour? When you have filled in every time slot from the moment you awoke to the moment you got back into bed, take a look back at it.

What do you notice?

Is your day filled with all the things you want to do, that make you feel alive and lead you towards your goals? Or is the day filled with the things you have to do and the things you think you ought to do?

When my clients complete this activity, they find they spend a lot of time doing nothing, or things that waste their time. They find they are not being very productive as a result. For example, they spend all evening in front of the TV and they check their email at regular intervals throughout the day. They also tend to find that they are filling their day with things that aren't going to lead them towards their goals and desires in life or that they are giving away their time too freely.

**What I Like List**

Now, write a list of the things that you would like to do. What are the things you think about but don't do? It may be that you have a musical instrument lying around and you just don't get the time to pick it up. Or maybe you want to write a short story? Or maybe you like to cook for friends? You may like to have holistic treatments.

Write down all the things that you like to do, that make you feel alive, that make you laugh and you feel satisfaction from. When you have your list, take a look and think about how often you do these things. Which of these would you like to do more of? Put a time frame next to the activities you list. What can you do in 5 minutes, 15 minutes, 30 minutes, an hour, half a day and a full day? Keep this list to hand and when you have free time, take a look at it to remind you of the things you could do. Choose one and do it!

## How to Take Time Out for You

Identify 3 things that you did yesterday that you can easily leave out of your day or tweak slightly.

Identify 3 things you want to do instead. These could be things that make you feel alive, make you laugh, take you one step further to your goals, help you relax or give you some space away from all the noise around you. They could be things from your list of things you like to do.

Replace the 3 things you don't want with the 3 things you do want. How will you make these changes?

Schedule time for you into your day. Think about it the day before so you can plan it in. What time could you take time out, around all the other things that are going on? How will you spend this time? For some it might be that they want to exercise. For others it may be they want to sit with a good book and relax for a while.

Limit the time you spend at a computer, in your own time. The internet and social media sites are a key time waster. It is so easy to search for information, gadgets and interesting things these days on the internet. Unfortunately, once you start looking it is a little bit addictive! It is seen as a tool to relax. However, you will find that if you turn it off and do something such as having a bath, reading a book or listening to music, you will relax far more than if you were sat at a computer screen. Try it and see for yourself.

Delegate your tasks at home to your partner and children if you can. This will not only spread the load but also make sure you have a little more time to yourself.

Don't be afraid to say no. If you have scheduled time in for you and someone wants you to do something, think about whether you want to do this thing. Are you just saying yes to please them? What would be the consequences of saying no to their request? Will this contribute to your goals? Now, a word of warning here. It is good to do things for others. Always think before you say yes or no. Don't say no until you have thought about it. If you can do it without too much interruption, then do it.

Get up a little earlier. I know, this sounds crazy…. But, if you get up just a little before everyone else, you will have some time all to yourself!

Get moving in your lunch break. So many people sit and eat at their desk while on the computer (many using the internet!). You have a lunch break. Use it! Take the time to go and get outside in the fresh air. Which of those activities you love can you do in your lunch break?

Find opportunities for quiet time. If you commute, instead of turning on the radio or making a phone call, turn everything off and enjoy the quiet. If you have children, introduce a quiet hour where they play quietly while you rest and relax. Turn the radio off. Turn the TV off. Turn off the computer. Tune into the quiet and peace around you for a while. Listen to the natural sounds all around you – the birds tweeting or the wind in the trees.

We all need a little time every day to recharge, refresh and reflect on what is going on around us. This time out will be exactly what you need to make sure you get back into things feeling more alive and ready for what is ahead. It will also help to manage stress, make you more productive throughout the day and will improve your relationships and mood. You will notice you become happier, more positive and feel more in balance.

Try not to get caught up in the hustle and bustle of everyday life. Whatever it is you like to do, just make sure you are taking time for you every day to do it.

Get in to the habit of thinking, how will I spend my time for me today? What can I do to make my spirit feel alive?

# Chapter 27: Leave Your Ego at the Door

**The ego.** A strange beast. The ego is practical. It is protective. It is judgemental and cautious. Your ego likes to think it is in charge.

I like to think of the ego as a little goblin figure who sits on my shoulder. He is called Bob. Bob wears an earthy coloured toga and has a fork in his hand. His toga is torn in places and he is a little overweight. He is heavy on my shoulder. He has a frown permanently plastered across his face. He carries a plain and ordinary food fork. He wants me to survive and will do everything he can to make sure I do, after all, the world is such a nasty place, right?

Bob is the one that sits and tells me what I should be doing. If I don't listen, he tries to stab me in the face with his fork. He is a destructive little goblin. He sees everyone as competition and every conversation is a potential argument to him. He fears everything, from being hurt to being exposed in some form. He is hard to quieten down and stomps up a fuss whenever he can see an appropriate moment. He frequently blames others, makes excuses and criticises everything and everyone. His main aim is to be safe. And he will do ANYTHING to make sure he is. I associate Bob with the mind.

**The spirit.** Spirit on the other hand is everything little Bob isn't. Spirit is free, it is loving, it is creative, it is light and it is playful. It is expressive and abundant. It is much more powerful than Bob. When I am living in spirit, I am being guided in a calm way through all the new, exciting and challenging experiences. It is wise and is associated with intuition, love, joy, peace and inspiration. I know when I am living in spirit because I feel serene, connected to the world and I feel centred. I am able to express myself in a more loving way and life flows easily. There are no struggles, no battles and no forks in my face. I feel surrounded by a lovely energy that makes me feel happy and smiley. I associate spirit with the heart.

## Over to You

Think for yourself now. Can you identify the two elements to your being? Do you recognise the ego and when it is in full swing? Do you recognise the spirit and the ease you feel when you are living in spirit?

Ego makes us feel, think and act in a very different way to spirit. Everything feels like a struggle with Bob in tow. Living in ego pulls your energy right down. It makes you be a person you don't want to be. Spirit makes you feel alive and connected to everyone and everything.

Ego makes people do strange things. I'm sure you will have seen someone who feels threatened in some way speaking from ego. It is very clear to see and can get quite messy at times. When your ego is playing out, you won't be your true self. Your true self is spirit and would like to come out to play more often than ego. However the ego is strong and will fight back spirit whenever it can.

For you to achieve health, happiness and get the most of yourself, I suggest you leave your ego at the door. Now, this isn't easy.

First of all, you need to be aware of when your ego is at play. How do you think, act and feel when your ego is in full swing? Note down these things so you can learn to identify it more clearly.

I gave my ego a name. I did this so it would make it more real to me. I also pictured how he would look and his mannerisms. Putting a name and a face on it makes it easier for me to stop Bob in his tracks when he starts. I picture him and tell him to 'stop right there'.

When your ego starts to come out, be aware of it as soon as you can. Making the list of how you feel, think and act will help with this. Once you are aware, you can challenge it and stop it from taking over.

Challenge it by living in spirit more often. Do this by living in the present, take responsibility for your actions (instead of blaming and accusing others) and choose to think positively and in the higher vibrational frequencies (such as love, joy, gratitude and peace). Quieten your mind as often as you can by using meditation or any alternative method. This links you to spirit and helps you to access wisdom.

Know what your spirit looks, feels and acts like. When you know this, you will recognise it more easily. What does your spirit love? Do things frequently that make your spirit soar and feel alive.

Really connect with your spirit and do things that nourish it every day.

I could talk all day about this, but I am going to stop there and refer you to another book on the subject. Sonia Choquette wrote an amazing book entitled 'The Answer is Simple… Love Yourself, Live Your Spirit'. In it she talks all about the spirit and how to recognise, connect and be one with your spirit. I highly recommend reading it if this is of interest to you.

## Chapter 28: Put More Fun into Your Life

Do you have fun? Would you say that you are happy? Do you go about your daily tasks with a spring in your step? If not, why not?! It is your right to experience these things.

What do you think happiness is? Can you define it? Note down your thoughts.

"Happiness does not depend on what you have or who you are. It solely relies on what you think."
Buddha.

Happiness is a state of mind that can be changed. It is not a permanent state by any means. It is something that you are and you feel. It starts from the way that you think. If you think negatively, you will feel low in energy and sluggish. You will probably be feeling angry, sad, pessimistic and anxious. If you think positively and have an optimistic view of life, you will experience all the higher vibrational energies, such as love, happiness and peace.

Having fun and experiencing happiness is vital to you living a balanced, healthier and happier lifestyle. Without it, you will be miserable and people won't want to spend time with you. You will be exuding all those low vibrational energies and people will dodge you rather than opt to spend time with you. You will also start to see pains, aches and illnesses if you keep living within this low frequency. Having fun will help to manage stress and will give you a different perspective on life.

## Over to You

Think back to a time when you experienced happiness and fun. When I say this to my clients, they often take me back to their childhood. A time where they had no responsibilities and commitments and could just be free. I know when I think of a time when I was truly happy, I remember playing in the fields across the road from my house with my brothers. Hide and seek was a firm favourite as was riding my bike across the hills. I remember feeling free and laughing so much, until my belly hurt. How did you feel at this time? Can you remember what you were thinking? Or how you were acting?

Can you think of a time when you were having fun or happy that is more recent than childhood? It may be a struggle but there will be times when you had fun, laughed and were fully engaged in what you were doing. Our busy lives cloud these memories a little, but they are there.

I remember going to Go Ape for a birthday in my 20s with a few friends. We had such a great time playing in the trees and enjoyed a picnic afterwards. I remember the feeling of warmth in my belly and laughing so much. I remember going home feeling love and very light in my body.

What times do you remember? Make a note of these as you remember them. Look back at them when you are looking for inspiration or want to remember happy times.

**Put Fun in Your Life**
Here are a few thoughts on how to put more fun into your life.

Think of all the things that make you laugh, smile, make you happy and make you feel good. This may be things you do now or things that you have done in the past. It may even go as far back as your childhood. What about hopscotch, climbing trees or walking in rivers? Take a piece of paper and write these things down.

Now, look at the list. Which of these do you do now? Which haven't you done for a while? What could you do to bring more fun and happiness into your life? How will you do this?

Find opportunities to laugh as much as you can. This may be through comedy, films, music, books or spending time with friends and family. Laugh at yourself too. Laughing opens the heart and awakens the spirit. Learn to lighten up and laugh as often as you can.

Enjoy every moment you experience by living in the present.

Find fun and happiness in the simple things in life. I try to have fun when I am doing all of the household jobs, as they can drag your energy down if you let them. When ironing, I put on some music so I can sing along and enjoy the experience. When I am walking somewhere, I make sure I look around and see the beauty in my surroundings. If I see children playing or animals on my travels, I stop and enjoy the noise and picture in front of me. This makes me smile.

Think of all the things that you do. If there are particular things that you really don't enjoy doing, either delegate them or find a way to make it more enjoyable.

Think about children for just a moment. We can learn a lot from children. They live in the moment, they are keen to learn new things all the time and they notice nature. They can describe to you what a beetle and a dandelion looks like in the finest of detail. They smile a lot more than adults and can find the beat to music and start to dance to it within seconds. They are great at taking themselves out of their comfort zone and living through it. They climb, jump, skip and run over anything and everything. They give high fives to anyone they think deserves one. They love to create; be it a picture, building something or writing. They use their imaginations freely and without sensor. They get dirty and don't care. And they break rules. How could you take some of this and use it in your life to have more fun?

# Chapter 29: Lift Your Mood

Moods are a funny old thing. Sometimes you may be in a fantastic mood. Other times you may be in a foul mood and anyone that comes into contact with you could be in real danger! You may even be in a great mood and then all of a sudden, something switches you into being a raging monster. Moods are most certainly not a permanent thing, they can change so quickly.

You can choose your moods. Moods are a state of mind. You can choose whether you are miserable about something all day. Or you can choose not to let whatever has upset, annoyed or frustrated you to bother you. You can choose to be happy and smile all day. You have the choice. Which will you choose?

Health wise, if you are regularly in a low mood you are more prone to poor health and a lower quality of life. You are also more likely to have health issues such as high blood pressure and heart disease. If you are regularly in a good mood, you will enjoy a better quality of life as well as feeling and looking healthy.

## How to Lift Your Mood
Be aware of your thoughts. When you sense a negative spell coming on, stop the thoughts before they take hold.

If you find yourself in an argument or stressful situation, take yourself out of it for a few moments. Give yourself a few minutes to put things into perspective and go back in smiling.

Visualise yourself in a good mood, laughing and enjoying yourself.

Exercise.

Socialise with others. This lifts the spirit and raises your mood considerably. Why not phone someone, meet up with someone or go and do something together?

Think positively and try to see the good in everything. If something negative happens, think about why this might have happened? For example, if you didn't get the job you went for, consider if you are ready for it. Things happen for a reason and I can guarantee there is something just around the corner that is much more suited to you.

Get a good night's sleep.

Get out into the sun and fresh air.

Put flowers and plants around the house. This will raise the quality of the air in your home and brighten your spirit.

If you have a pet, play with it. Tug of war with a dog is a fantastic way to make you smile and laugh out loud.

Do something to make you smile. Whatever makes you smile, do it.

Get creative – cook, draw, sing or make something.

Use these ideas to get you in the best possible mood you can be in. Take time to recognise your moods and what shifts you into the lower vibrational moods. When you know the triggers, you can start to work to eliminate them from your life. Remember that you choose your moods. So choose only the best.

## Chapter 30: Do You Value Yourself?

Most of us undervalue ourselves. We hear that it is bad to think highly of ourselves. It is seen to be arrogant to think this way. The thing is, if you don't value yourself, others won't value you either. Others will treat you how you treat yourself. And if you value yourself, you will be happier.

We all bring something different to this world and this life.

## Over to You

Think now for a moment about what you bring. Start off by writing a list of all the things that you bring to this world. It might be that you are a loyal friend or that you have a good sense of humour that lightens the mood. Write down everything that you think is valuable about you. Take a look at this list a day later and add more to it. Keep adding to this list for a few days until you are sure you have everything down there that you value about yourself. If you want another perspective on you, ask a close friend or family what they value about you. This activity is great to get you thinking about you, your qualities, what you are good at and what you bring to the people around you.

**Ask yourself these questions too and note the responses.**

What are you good at? Write down everything you think you are good at. Everything. Think about your home life, your social life, your work life, you as a person.

Then think about all the things you like about you. It could be your personality, your looks, your habits, your quirks, your energy. List everything you like about you.

Keep taking a look at your answers to these two questions. If you are ever in need of a pick me up, some confidence or are looking for a change in direction, look back at the lists you have compiled. I regularly look at my lists and update them, tweak them and refer to them when I reach a crossroads. You will find them useful in lots of areas of your life, I guarantee.

### How to Value Yourself More

There are many things you can do to value yourself more. Start off with the activities above. Then try some or all of these.

- Think positively.
- See your mistakes as a learning opportunity, and not something to hit yourself across the face with every day.
- Surround yourself with positive people.
- Set small, achievable goals. Achieving them will make you feel great.
- Notice all the little things you do to help others. Do nice things for others.
- Stop comparing yourself to other people.
- Stop trying to be 100% perfect all the time. Settle with 80%.

It would be really useful for you to get to know yourself a little better. When you know who you truly are, where you are heading and what you have to offer, you will enjoy life more.

### Want to Know Yourself Better?

Answer these questions:

- Who are you? A mother, a wife... List everything that you are.
- What do you want?
- What do you need?
- What do you like to do?
- What do you need to learn?

- What do you need to do to simplify your life?
- What can you let go of that is holding you back or keeping you in the past?
- What do you want to have done, achieved and be in your life?
- What are your unhelpful thoughts?
- What do you believe?
- What needs to happen for you to live the life you want?
- What would you do if you weren't afraid?
- What makes you truly happy in your life?
- What areas of your life would you most like to change?

Once you have the answers to these, you will have a better understanding of who you are as a person and what you want out of your life. When you have a clear purpose you can start to plan your journey. Only when you truly know who you are and what you want can you start to live your life purposefully.

# Chapter 31: How to Relax

How relaxed are you? Do you make it a priority to relax and unwind every day? If not, you might want to think about how you can do this. Relaxation is perhaps one of the single most important aspects to achieving great health and wellbeing. When we relax, our body has the opportunity to unwind and all the stresses of the day flow away from the body.

The benefits of relaxation have been well researched and published worldwide. It has been proven to give the heart a rest by slowing down the heart rate. It reduces blood pressure and slows the rate of breathing, which reduces the need for oxygen. It increases blood flow to the muscles and decreases muscle tension.

As a result of relaxation on a regular basis, many people experience more energy, better sleep, enhanced immunity, less headaches and pain and smoother emotions (less anger, crying, anxiety or frustration). Many people also see increased concentration, better problem-solving abilities and greater efficiency overall.

When you relax fully, how does it make you feel? Do you notice a change in your thoughts, feelings and behaviour? Do you notice these changes straight away, straight after or for days/weeks afterwards? What were you doing to achieve this state of relaxation?

Think of all the times when you felt truly relaxed. What were you doing? Make a note of these things.

If you build relaxation into every day and you make it a priority, you will start to notice the longer-term benefits it can give to you. Relaxing as a one off makes you feel great, right at that moment. But within hours you will notice that the benefits have passed and you are back to yourself. Relaxing on an ongoing basis will help you to reap the full physical, emotional and spiritual benefits that will last and enable you to live within spirit (and not ego).

Many people are unsure about how to relax and unwind. With busy home lives, careers and social lives, it can be difficult to fit everything you want into a day. When time is limited, it can be difficult to prioritise yourself and your needs. It is easy to feel guilty for allowing yourself to take time out when there is so much to be done. There is a perception that taking time out makes you weak and a failure of some kind. Actually, quite the opposite is true. If you don't give yourself time to relax and unwind, you are opening yourself up to illness, poor mental health and are less likely to be successful.

Giving yourself time every day to relax will enable you to reach your full potential, while giving you time and space to unwind and take a step back from everything.

We are at our most creative when we are relaxed. How many times have you been struggling with ideas on a particular thing, only for the ideas to flow in abundance when you are on holiday and away from it all? I can't begin to tell you how often this happens to me. My most creative moments are when I am relaxed and enjoying myself. Some of my most inspired moments have been while I am away in the campervan or walking up a hill with friends.

Giving yourself this time and distance from situations will give you the space you need to let your subconscious guide you. Why would you feel guilty about allowing that process to happen?

## How to Relax

Let us look at different strategies to help you to relax. I ask that you keep an open mind as you read these. You might want to try a few of these or all of them. You decide.

First and foremost, build relaxation into your day. Don't make it something that you do if you have the time. Make it a priority, just like cooking the tea or getting into work for 9am. If you plan ahead and look at when you may be able to have some down time, you will not only look forward to it but also get rid of any guilty feelings when you do take the time out.

Let go of any guilt you may be nurturing around relaxing. When you engage in relaxation, if you feel guilty about taking the time, you won't enjoy it and you will spend more time winding yourself up than relaxing. Decide that you will relax and switch your mind off. Enjoy the time that you have.

Think of all the things you do that make you feel relaxed. For me, it is something creative. Playing my guitar or cooking really help me to relax and unwind. What do you do that makes you feel relaxed and at ease within yourself? Keep a note of these things and when you are ready to relax and take time out, look at what helps you to relax. Think about engaging in different activities throughout the week.

Pamper yourself. This might mean taking a long soak in a hot bath with a good book. It might mean that you put a face mask on and listen to soothing music. It might even mean that you book in for a massage. Whatever you choose to do, do it guilt free.

Try self-massage. Give your hands and feet a massage. This will help to release tension that has been building up throughout the day and will make them feel light and great.

Light some candles to create a soft and calming atmosphere. Turn off the 'big light'.

Put some soothing music on in the background.

Curl up on the sofa or your bed with a good book.

If you have a pet, cuddle them, stroke them and give them some of your love. Hearing a cat purr can transform you from a raging monster into the serene person that is within.

Use fragrances such as aromatherapy oils. Burn these in an oil burner to release the aromas. Different oils have different properties and stimulate different responses. Lavender is the most well-known and widely available oil to help relax your body and mind. Look for alternative oils you can use and blend together to create the desired effects. There are many good books on this subject.

Don't watch the clock. This will only stress you out and ensure you don't enjoy the time you have. If you need to be somewhere or do something at a certain time, consider setting an alarm and putting it somewhere away from you so you can focus on just being in the moment. That way you won't be late but will also not be clock watching the whole time.

Practice breathing exercises. Concentrate on your breathing and nothing else. This will not only bring you into the present moment but will also slow down your breathing and help you to relax your body and mind.

Close your eyes for a moment.

Try to release the tension within your body. Start at your head and work your way down the body, slowly. Tense up your forehead and then relax. Tense your jaw and relax. Do this all the way down your body, right down to the tip of your toes.

Engage in activities that take your mind off of daily life.

Think about the things you enjoy. This might be creating something (drawing, painting, cooking, sewing, creating Lego castles, music), a sporting activity (fishing, swimming, golf, kicking a football around), taking photographs or growing something. Whatever it might be, enjoy it and live in the moment.

Look for opportunities to smile and laugh. Do this as often as you can in your day.

Limit the time you spend with people that stress you out, have a negative outlook or are critical. Instead, surround yourself with people that exude love, peace and are positive.

Turn off all technological devices and put them away. This can be very difficult to do but I guarantee you will feel refreshed and grounded if you do. I do this on evenings when I have been at a computer all day. I leave my mobile phone in another room (to avoid the internet and social media temptation). I put computers out of the lounge and leave the TV switched off. I light a few candles, burn a little oil and grab a good book to settle down with. When I go to bed, I notice I am totally relaxed. My body and mind feel light and I always sleep soundly as a result. Try it and see what effect it has on you.

Look out of the window for 5 minutes. See what is going on all around you.

Practice meditation. I will talk about this in a few moments.

Don't forget, when you are doing all of these things, to live in the present moment.

You may already do some of these things and know they work for you. Why not try out a few different ones to see if you can spice up your relaxation time a little and to add some variety into your life.

# Chapter 32: Explore Meditation

Meditation is a powerful tool for relaxation and is an extremely effective way to relax, switch off and de-stress. Many people are unsure what meditation is and how to do it. They think it is something that Tibetan monks do, high up in the mountains to reach Nirvana. They assume they spend many long hours sat in silence with their legs crossed in the lotus position. Would it surprise you if I said, people just like you do this every day? Minus the mountains, long hours and lotus position.

Before we look at how to meditate, let us first look at the reasons for meditating. Do you have a million and one thoughts rushing around in your head all day long? Do you constantly hear the internal chatter in your mind? Are you unsure of which direction to take or just want a breather from day to day life? Meditation is an opportunity to quieten the mind.

There are many different reasons for engaging in meditation. For some people, they simply want to relax and switch off. This benefit of meditation is self-evident. For others, meditation is part of a spiritual journey and is more about expansion of awareness, communicating with the spirit and exploring how they perceive and experience life.

Others are interested in the benefits of meditation for their health and general wellbeing. Regular meditation has been documented as having major health benefits over the years. These include lowering the blood pressure, encouraging better sleep and decreasing anxiety levels. It encourages a faster healing time and a decreased use of drugs, alcohol and cigarettes. It helps to lower cholesterol and build a stronger immune response. It also reduces stress hormones, which in itself brings many benefits.

The effectiveness of meditation comes from deep relaxation. When we are deeply relaxed, the body and mind are refreshed and revitalized. This brings many benefits that are both immediate and long lasting. The key here is to engage in regular meditation.

There are many different ways to meditate. You need to find the way that works for you. The traditional way to meditate is by sitting and taking time out. If you don't like to sit still, you might find that activities such as walking in nature, listening to music or knitting are just what you need instead. The most important thing is to actually take some time from your day to devote to meditation.

An easy way to begin with meditation is by using guided meditations. You can get hold of these in word, audio or visual form. Your local library will stock a selection or you can get hold of them very easily on the internet. They aren't expensive and will give you an introduction to meditation. Deepak Chopra regularly runs 21-day meditation challenges that can be accessed via Facebook. These are good for beginners. You might find a meditation group in your local area too.

So let me take you through how to meditate, if you choose the sitting type of meditation.

**Simple Meditation**
Firstly, find a quiet space where you can sit for a while and where you won't get disturbed. If you need to put a sign on the door or take yourself away somewhere else, do it. Do whatever you need to do to make sure you have a quiet space and to know you won't get disturbed.

Get comfortable in a seated position. Make sure your feet are firmly on the floor and your back is supported. You may need to add padding behind you to make sure you can touch the floor and are supported appropriately. I use cushions. Drop your chin slightly so your spine is straight and lengthened. Make sure your legs are not crossed and your hands are in your lap, either face up or face down. Don't cross your hands over.

When you are comfortable and ready, close your eyes. Start by breathing slowly and deeply in and out through your nose. Focus on your breathing and notice how your breath feels when you breathe in and out. Do you feel the rising of your chest as you breathe in? Can you feel the air moving in and out of your nose?

Think about the tension you feel in your body. Wherever you feel this tension, as you breathe out imagine that you are breathing out this tension with the out breath. You are breathing in pure healing energy and breathing out the tension that has accumulated. Let it flow from your body.

When you have released all the tension and your body feels relaxed, turn your attention again to your breathing. When your mind wanders to thoughts, bring it back to thinking about your breathing. If you need to process thoughts, that will happen. Just trust that what happens is right for you at the time.

Thoughts do arise spontaneously in the mind. They are a natural part of meditation. The goal of meditation is to become more at ease, relaxed and at peace with whatever is happening. Therefore, it is important to not resist anything that comes in meditation, including thoughts. Don't try to push out your thoughts or resist them. Simply notice that thoughts are present and let them go the way they come — effortlessly. When you find that your awareness has been caught up in a train of thought, easily come back to the focus of your meditation. It's important to understand that you have not made a mistake when thoughts come or the mind has become absorbed in thought. It is a natural part of meditation.

Also be aware that if you lie down (which your body associates with sleep) you may fall asleep! Trust that your body will do whatever it needs to in this time. If you need sleep, you will fall asleep. I try not to meditate in bed since my mind associates bed with sleep. Instead, I sit on a chair or the sofa in the lounge.

When you are ready to leave the meditation, take a few moments to come around. Start by hearing everything that is around you. Notice the sounds in your environment. Take a few deep breaths and bring your awareness back into your body. When you are ready, slowly open your eyes. Take a few moments before you start to move and become active again. You should notice that you feel relaxed and at peace.

This is a simple meditation that you can do at any time of day. If you want to relax, try this out every day.

**Spiritual Meditation**
Let me introduce you to a meditation that I find very beneficial, both for relaxing purposes and for connecting with my spirit. I was introduced to this by a lovely couple, Ann and Jonathan Halstead. They help people to awaken their psychic abilities and to connect with their spirit.

Take the steps above to quieten the mind. Once you have released the tension and are feeling relaxed focus on your breathing for a few moments. Get into a regular breathing pattern that feels comfortable for you.

Then start to open up the chakras. Do this by visualising the following.

Start at the root chakra, which is located at the base of your spine. Here visualise a spinning disc, vortex whirling around or something associated with the colour red. As it whirls around notice the colour and the way it pulses out into your aura. I imagine a red rose opening up and the colour spreading out into my auric field.

Move up to the sacral chakra, located in your lower abdomen. Here visualise a spinning disc, vortex or object that is orange in colour whirling around. Notice that as it spins or opens it pulses out orange into your aura. I imagine I am peeling an orange and as I do, the orange juice squirts out into my auric field.

Move on up to the solar plexus chakra, located in your upper abdomen area. Here the spinning disc, vortex or object is yellow and as it spins it pulses out yellow into your aura. I imagine a sunrise and the yellow gliding across the air out into my auric field.

Next is the heart chakra, located in the centre of your chest. Here the spinning disc, vortex or object is green. Imagine it is pulsing out the green colour into the aura. I imagine here that I am running through a field of long green grass that is as tall as me and the green is absorbed into my aura.

Move up to the throat chakra, located in your throat area. Here the spinning disc, vortex or object is sky blue. It pulses out the sky blue colour into the aura. I imagine I have just opened the curtains to reveal a beautiful summers day. The sky is clear and as I open the curtains, the colour spreads out into my aura.

Then move up to the third eye chakra. This is located on your forehead, between your eyes. Here the spinning disc, vortex or object is an indigo colour and it pulses out indigo into the aura. I imagine blueberries and as I bite into them the juice sprays into my auric field.

Finish off with the crown chakra, which is located at the very top of your head towards the back. Here the spinning disc, vortex or object is a beautiful violet colour. As it spins it pulses out the beautiful violet colour into the aura. I imagine a piece of amethyst crystal. When the sun hits it the violet rays beam out into my auric field.

Sit for a while as you notice all these colours circulating in your aura and combine to create a rainbow.

Draw your attention to the top of your head again. Notice a beam of light coming down through the top of your head. As you breathe in, you breathe in this pure white light. As you breathe out, you breathe it into all parts of your body. As you continue to do this, your body is filled with white light and it starts to spread out into your aura. It fills your aura and feels cleansing and you feel light.

As you sit and enjoy this pureness, mentally invite your spirit guides to come and sit with you for a while in this space you have created. Invite them to enjoy the energy you have created. Sit now and enjoy the light. If they want to communicate with you, ask them to do it now. Look out for any visuals, audio you might hear or sensations in your body. That is their way of communicating with you.

When you are ready to leave this place, thank your spirit guides for sitting with you and ask them to step back now.

Breathe in and as you do so, imagine the white light coming in through the top of your head and flowing out through your feet and fingers. Let it wash through you. When you are ready, start to close down the chakras. Start with the crown chakra and imagine the spinning disc (or alternative) coming to a standstill or that it closes up nice and tight. Work your way down the chakras, closing them down as you go. Work down from the crown, to the third eye, to the throat, to the heart, to the solar plexus, to the sacral and finish off with the root chakra.

Focus your attention on your feet now. Feel roots growing from your feet and spreading down into the ground. Feel roots coming up from the ground and pulling your feet closer to it. As you become grounded, bring your attention back into your body.

Slowly, start to come around. Notice the sounds around you and when you are ready open your eyes. Take a few moments to come around before you start to move and be active.

Have a notepad beside you and as you come around, note down any thoughts, visions, noises or feelings you had while you were in your meditation. You may have noticed the chakras felt to have different energies. The root chakra may have been spinning very slowly and felt dense whereas the crown chakra may have been spinning much faster and felt incredibly light. This is normal and shows that each chakra has a life of its own! Using this meditation is a really great way to relax, connect with spirit and clear any blockages you had in the chakras. How do you feel afterwards?

I make the point of meditating in this way every day. As a result, I feel at peace within myself and am better able to cope with anything that comes my way. I deal with situations in a calm way and feel in control of my body and mind at all times.

Give mediation a go. It really can change your outlook and your life.

## Chapter 33: The Power of Visualisation

You may have heard the term visualisation. Do you know what it actually means and the power of it?

Visualising means seeing something clearly in your mind's eye. Close your eyes for a minute. Think of your front door. What do you see? How does it look? Are there any distinguishing features on it? What is it made out of? What is the texture like? Is it warm or cold to touch? Is there any glass on it? If so, what does it look like? Now go outside and take a look at it. How did you do?

When you did that, you may have experienced something completely different to someone else who looked at the exact same door. People visualise in different ways. Some people close their eyes and actually see a picture. For others they imagine it. Some see in colour, others see in black and white. Some see shapes, others see a scene unfolding in front of their eyes. For some the picture is still, like a photograph. For others, it is moving, like a film.

Visualisation has proven to be extremely successful in producing a specific outcome, the one that is seen in the mind's eye. Studies have shown that the brain doesn't know the difference between what is real and what is imagined. Your conscious mind doesn't differentiate between what is a real event and what is a 'made up' event. It will seek to play out that which you see. The conscious mind believes that the successful result you envisage has already happened and acts accordingly.

Remember when I said earlier that how you choose to speak to yourself and the images you allow to impress upon your mind have a direct connection to your outward experience? This is the power of visualisation.

So what are the benefits of visualising? There are so many different benefits and advantages to visualising. I will outline a few key ones below.

Relaxation and stress relief. The simple act of quietening your mind and visualising something (whatever that may be) reduces the amount of stress you are constantly bombarded with on a daily basis. It gives you quiet space and time to think about the life you want to lead. Because you are relaxed, it also gives you the health and wellbeing benefits that this brings.

Visualising something that you want to have or want to experience can bring great joy into your life. We may not be in the position right now to do or have exactly what we want, but we can visualise it, and your mind will respond in the same way as if you were actually experiencing it. This is the next best thing to actually having it or doing it, as our minds don't know the difference between that which is real and that which is imagined.

Since your thoughts become your reality, you can shape your life into whatever you choose it to be. If you can imagine it, you can create it. Don't forget that your life at the present moment is largely the result of what you have visualised up to this point. However, if you are like most people, you have created results without realising you are doing so. Be aware that this unlimited power is within your hands and you can begin to create by conscious and deliberate choice, rather than by unconscious default.

With visualisation, the sky is your limit. If you can see it, you can achieve it. If you feel stuck in a rut, whether it be in your job or a relationship, visualisation is the key to getting you unstuck. When you can imagine your life as you wish it to be and you feel the reality of its presence now, it is only a matter of time before it becomes your reality.

Take charge of your life. It is your life after all and you are the one that can take it to where you want it to go. Remember that you hold the key to all of your experiences, creations, accumulations and achievements, whatever they may be. The power is within you. Create the life you want in your mind and it will soon become a reality.

I firmly believe in the power of visualisation and that what you imagine, you can create. Here is a personal example of visualisation at work. In 2011, I decided that I wanted to become self-employed and leave my full-time employment behind. I started to visualise the outcome I wanted and asked for guidance on how to achieve this. Step by step I was offered the guidance on how to achieve my vision through meditation and over time I started to see my vision playing out in front of me. The journey was slightly different to what I had initially imagined but I can honestly say I am now on the right path. My spirit stepped in and helped me to see the opportunities that were being presented to me and as a result, I am living my vision. It hasn't been an easy journey and I needed to develop a lot of skills and personal qualities to take this path. I can say though, that I have enjoyed every step I have taken to get to where I am now.

**How to Visualise**
First you must decide exactly what you want. If you don't know, I suggest you get clear, because if you don't know what you want, how can you expect to get it?

Get the piece of paper out from the 'Value Yourself' section with the answer to 'what I want' on it. Look down this list. Strike out anything that you no longer want. Focus on one aspect of what you want. Clearly define exactly what it is you want.

If, for instance, you want to be self-employed, write down exactly what this means to you. What are you doing? How many hours do you work? Who do you work with? What are you helping them with? What do you do day to day?

Make sure you are very clear and specific about what it is you want. Write down every little detail about it; how it will look, feel, what you will hear and how things around you will be changed. Really put a lot of thought into this and get down every single detail on paper.

When you have this on paper and firmly in your mind, you must practice creating the desired outcome (in your mind) on a daily basis.

Get comfortable, be it sitting or lying down. You may even prefer to visualise as you are doing something, such as walking. Close your eyes and start to relax your body and mind. Slow your breathing and take some time to relax fully. Follow the simple meditation if this helps.

When you are relaxed and are ready to begin, see yourself being successful at whatever it is you want. Imagine the end result you want to have. Imagine what you are doing, who you are with, what you are feeling, what you are saying, what you can smell and what you are hearing all around you. Imagine the person you have become. Imagine it as though it were actually happening to you right now. Imagine achieving your goals as vividly as you can. Try to intensify the feelings, visions and thoughts you are having. Imagine being happy and healthy as a result of all of that you see. See the event happening in your mind and imagine it exactly how you want it to play out. Take note of everything you see, hear, feel and think in this time.

To accelerate the manifestation of your goals, it is really important to feel the emotions that you would feel, as if it were a reality right now. Seeing the pictures is not enough. The pictures will show you what to look out for on the journey but you also need to show your mind which feelings it needs to look out for too. Bring forward the emotions you think you will feel when it becomes a reality. Really feel everything about the experience. Try to intensify these feelings as much as you can. These emotions will filter into your subconscious mind and help to generate results much faster.

When you are ready to come out of the visualisation, take a few deep breaths. Slowly bring your awareness back to your body and when you are ready, open your eyes. Take a moment to rest before becoming active again.

Remember when you are visualising to visualise the whole picture. Don't just think about one or two elements of it. Really imagine how this would affect your whole life and the people around you. Imagine it in as much detail as you can.

Consider if you need to work on any aspects of yourself to ensure you can have the things you want. Write down anything that you might need to work on and formulate a plan to ensure you become this person that is prepared for your visions.

This visualization time allows you to really connect with your goal. See it and feel it, because it is yours. Enjoy visualising what you want. It can be fun and very uplifting if you let it.

The more often you can do this the better. Repeating the images regularly will allow them to flow into the subconscious mind, which will begin the process of manifesting. It is no good just doing this once. This will not create a lasting impression on your subconscious. Repeat this a few times a week. And don't forget to acknowledge when opportunities come your way, as these are the start of your visions turning into reality.

# Chapter 34: Appreciate all the Good in Your Life

What does gratitude mean to you? When I think of gratitude, I think of taking notice of all the simple pleasures in my life, of being thankful and acknowledging everything that I receive. When I am thankful, my focus shifts from that of lack to all of the abundance that is around me. I am shifted from a place of lower frequency energy to those light and uplifted energies instead. When you say thanks and mean it, do you notice a shift in your energy? Next time you give thanks, note how it makes you feel.

Let's face it. We all like to be thanked. It's a great feeling to have someone, especially someone who doesn't stand to gain anything from us, tell us that we made a difference in their lives. When you thank someone, have you noticed how it illuminates them and lifts them to a frequency of love and pleasure?

The feeling of gratitude and appreciation opens the heart and quietens the mind, so how could it not be good for you?

Studies have shown that it improves the overall quality of life. Keeping an attitude of gratitude benefits both your physical and your mental health. Showing your gratitude produces good feelings, it helps you to relax and creates happier memories. It makes you healthier and deepens relationships. You become kinder, more social and have more friendships. You see an increase in productivity, you achieve more of your goals and you notice an improvement in your decision-making capabilities. You notice better management of your time. You become more spiritual, have increased self-esteem and are more optimistic. You are less materialistic, more active and as a result have increased energy. You suffer from less illness, feel refreshed and see an improvement in your sleep.

Being grateful reminds you of all the positive things in your life. It reminds you of what is important and to say thanks to others. It will help you to focus on all the good in the day and take the focus away from any negative experiences or thoughts you may be having. It will help you to put situations into perspective and realise what you have, instead of what you are lacking.

Take the time to appreciate all the good in your life.

## How to Give Thanks

It is so easy to pass by all the good things that have happened within your day, and to focus on the negativity instead. Here are a few ways for you to focus on the good things in your life and to give thanks.

Grab a pen and paper. Note down all the things that you are grateful for in your life. Make sure you note all of the things, people, feelings, achievements and opportunities that you are thankful for.

Keep a gratitude diary. Every day think of all the things you are grateful for, that have gone well, that you have enjoyed or appreciated. I do this every night before I sleep. That way I go to sleep on a happy note and am thinking of all the good things in my life. Don't forget the law of attraction; what you think about you will bring into your life. Doing this before you sleep will aid the thoughts to go into your subconscious mind. This will help to attract more of the same.

Take a few minutes each morning to give thanks to whoever or whatever you are grateful for. You can do this in your mind or out loud.

Commit to being grateful every day. Look for things that you really are grateful for and give thanks for it.

Give at least one compliment a day. It can be to a person or to show your appreciation of something (such as the quietness). When someone gives you a compliment, smile and say thank you. Don't shrug it off or ignore it.

Say thank you when someone does something nice for you, however small this may be. Make sure you mean it though. There is nothing worse than a forced and insincere thank you.

Call, email or write a note to say thanks if you remember something later on. Let them know you really appreciated it.

Write a letter to those that have had a positive influence on your life and those that you haven't properly thanked or acknowledged. Send it just because you can and not for any gain on your part.

Change your thoughts. Instead of focusing on the bad things that have happened, look for the good in the situation. Has it given you the feedback or opportunity to grow in any way? What are the possible reasons for this happening? What opportunities has it opened up for you? What can you learn from this?

Say thank you more often. Mean it when you say it.

Acknowledge one ungrateful thought every day and replace it with a grateful one.

Make the decision to not complain, criticise or gossip for 7 days. If you slip, take it on the chin and keep going. Don't beat yourself up about it. Notice at the end of the week the amount of energy you were giving to negative thoughts and actions.

Why not engage the rest of the family in this? When you are all sat together, ask what 3 things everyone is grateful for today. This is really good if someone has had a bad day; it helps to bring a different perspective and lift their mood.

Being grateful will shift your energy from the lower frequencies to those of love, light and peace. Make it a priority to be thankful every day for those things that make you smile and touch your life in a positive way.

## Chapter 35: Keep a Journal

Have you ever had so many thoughts whizzing around your head that you just thought you would explode? If you have ever written these thoughts, worries and concerns down on paper, you will have experienced a shift in your mind. You may have felt less anxious, worried and tense. You may even have noticed that the headache you have had for days disappeared. The act of writing down whatever was buzzing around in your head helps to gain clarity and a different perspective on things.

Journaling is the act of keeping a journal (a bit like a diary). In it, you write down and explore your thoughts and feelings surrounding the events of your life. It is good to keep a journal of all the positive things in your life as well as the negative aspects, to ensure you are not just focusing on the negative.

If you have ever seen the Harry Potter films, I like to think of journaling a bit like Albus Dumbledore's Pensieve.

Dumbledore uses the Pensieve to take the excess thoughts from his mind using his wand and places them in what looks to be a shallow stone basin filled with a cloudy liquid/gas. He reviews his memories so he can spot patterns and links as well as reliving all the emotions and feelings associated with it. Journaling is much the same as this, without the magic. Instead of using a wand, you would use a pen/pencil and write down all the thoughts around a particular time or event. Then you can gain the same benefits as Dumbledore. Now that is magic.

Why would you journal? The benefits of journaling have been widely researched and below I give you just a few of the key ones that resonate with me.

Journaling can clarify your thoughts and feelings. If you are ever unsure of what you want or feel take a few minutes to write down your thoughts and emotions surrounding that aspect of your life. This will quickly get you in touch with your inner voice and help you to process the thoughts and feelings you are having around it.

You will get to know yourself better. By writing regularly you will get to know what makes you feel happy and confident. You will also get to know which situations and people are not so good for you. This is all very important information for you to start taking control of your emotional wellbeing.

Journaling reduces stress. Writing about anger, sadness and any other painful emotions helps to release the intensity of these feelings. If you do this you will feel calmer and be better able to live and stay in the present moment.

You will be able to solve problems more effectively. Typically we problem solve from a left brained, analytical perspective. More often than not, the answer can only be found by engaging creativity and intuition (which is associated with the right brain). Free writing enables you to work through an issue or problem and helps to free up thinking so creativity can start to flow. You may find as a result that you come up with unexpected solutions to a problem you thought was very nearly unsolvable!

Journaling resolves disagreements with others. Writing about a misunderstanding rather than chewing it over in your head will help you to understand another person's point of view and perspective on the situation. By writing down all that happened and all the feelings and emotions you feel, you may come up with a sensible resolution to the conflict and disagreement.

## How to Journal

There are many different ways to journal. Here is the way that I find most beneficial for me. Experiment with different ways and find the way that works best for you.

First of all, get yourself a pen and a pad of paper or notebook.

Whenever you feel the need to get excess thoughts out of your head or you need to work through a thought or an issue, get this notebook out and sit somewhere comfortable. Some people like to journal when they are on their own so they don't get disturbed. Others do it while family are around. It is a very personal choice. Do whatever you feel is right.

You can journal as often or as little as you need to. It is up to you when, where and how you do it.

The key to journaling is to free write. This means that you just write and don't consciously form a piece of writing. Forget about all the conventions of writing well. Forget about the punctuation, grammar and spelling. Just write down freely whatever comes to mind. Don't sensor what you are writing. Write as though you know no one will see this. No one will see it so know that you won't be judged and you can say whatever you like during this time.

Some people worry that others may find it and read it. If this is the case, here are a few ideas for you. You could use just one piece of paper and write over and over the words you have already written. This will make the writing unreadable. You could also write and then destroy the paper by either ripping it up and putting it in the bin or burning it.

If you are going to use a notebook and will keep it, find somewhere you can put it that is away from eyes. Some of my clients keep it locked away somewhere. Others keep it in a drawer, wardrobe or cupboard. Find somewhere that you feel comfortable to leave it and know no one will come across it easily.

When you have reached a natural end to writing, put it away somewhere, or if you prefer, destroy it.

It is amazing how many times I have sat down, feeling anxious about something whilst having suffered from a headache for a few days. When I get my notebook out I have no idea what the issue is or what I am going to write. I sometimes even start off by writing, 'I have a headache and I have no idea why'. Then as I continue to write, just for the sake of continuing writing, all of a sudden I start to write about how I feel and before I know it, the issue comes out on to the paper right in front of me. I had no idea that this was an issue or that I had been thinking subconsciously about it. But it is there and as I write, I get all the emotion and feeling associated with it out. I always try once I have got all the emotion out, to write what I could do about it or learn from it for the future. At this point, ideas flood in that I had no idea I had and my creativity starts to kick in. My intuition starts to guide me and I am able to come up with really great ideas for moving me forward on it.

It is so easy, especially when you have a disagreement or feel let down in some way, to try to push it and the feelings to the back of your mind. I find when I do this that it comes back within a few days in a different way. Usually in the form of a persistent headache or other ache or pain in my body. When I journal and take the time to free write, not only does my head feel clearer and lighter and I feel lifted in some way, but I also find the headache or other pains disappear very quickly.

Sometimes, I know I need to journal straight away (and usually the emotions are quite raw at this stage) and other times I think I am fine with something and get on with living in the moment. However, this usually results in me journaling just a few days later. Sometimes the emotions are so raw that tears start to flow and other times I am looking at the page at amazing insight into something. This is all normal and you don't need to beat yourself up for not realising sooner that you would benefit from journaling. Just roll with it and when you do come round to do it, don't sensor anything. Get it all out. Only when you are uncensored and really get it out can you start to move on.

Does any of this sound familiar to you? Can you identify with the aches and pains that come on as a result of stress and anxiety around a situation? If you can, try journaling. It really is a powerful tool to help you to process, gain insight and see things from a different perspective. Grab yourself a pen and notebook and start writing. If you don't know what to write, write down the first words that come into your head or write what you see. Soon enough, your subconscious will take over and guide you to where you need to be.

Dumbledore is a very wise and emotionally intelligent wizard. He gives off an aura of serenity and composure and speaks in a very calm and collected way. We can learn a lot from him and you can choose to bring these qualities to yourself.

Journaling is a tool that will enable you to look within, connect with your inner voice and your internal guidance. Try it today to see the benefits for yourself.

## Chapter 36: Love Nature

Imagine for me this scene. It is a beautifully warm morning. The sun has just risen and is shining so brightly. You get out of bed, open the curtains and look out of the window. You feel happy and alive. You get dressed and head outside into the glorious summer day. As you walk across the fields of vibrant green, you feel the warmth of the sun on your face and as you feel it, you smile – both externally and internally. You breathe in the fresh air of the countryside and as you breathe in, you breathe in the aromas of freshly cut grass and the smell of the sweet flowers all around you. You feel light and alive.

Nice thought, yes? Can you take yourself back to a time when you went walking in the countryside, felt the warmth of the sun and smelt the aromas described? How did you feel during this time?

I remember a time when I was employed and had worked myself too hard for quite a long period of time. I went for a long weekend trip to Ingleborough in the Yorkshire Dales with my partner. We decided to walk up the mountain during the course of the weekend. I particularly remember feeling very stressed, uptight and thinking from ego predominantly in the lead up to the trip away. We set up camp in a tent near the base of Ingleborough where we intended to stay for a few nights. Unfortunately, it rained heavily for a few days which confined us to the inside of the tent for the majority of the time. At first, I remember feeling very annoyed and itching to get out and up the hill. We mainly sat and read, chatted and ate good food in these two days sat in the tent. The sound of the rain on the tent and the smell of the grass, rain and fresh air was very refreshing. We were immersed in nature. After sitting and chatting and just being for two days, I could feel the difference in my state of mind.

On the third day, the rain stopped and we could actually see the top of the mountain. We got up early, packed a bag full of food and warm clothes and headed up the mountain. It was a very long walk which took us most of the day. During this time we chatted, enjoyed the scenery and very much lived in the moment. Time passed very quickly and before we knew it, we were back at the bottom of the mountain feeling windswept but I had the biggest smile on my face. The fresh air and just being in nature really revived my spirit. It was exactly what I needed to bring me back into my body and take me out of my ego.

Can you relate to this and feeling this way? What was happening for you in the lead up? What did you see, do and hear to bring you back into living in spirit?

Being in the outdoors is one of the ways I use to bring me back to my spirit. It is one of the simplest things any of us can do. Yet, how often do you spend outside every week?

There is no better feeling than getting in touch with nature. There is so much to be experienced out in nature. You can listen to the birds, smell the different aromas given off by the trees and the vegetation all around. You can feel the wind and the heat of the sun on your skin. You can feel the earth and the grass under your feet. Do you notice these things when you are outside? Or are you more focused on getting to a destination or all the thoughts swimming around in your head?

If this sounds familiar, take some time out and get outside. Live in the moment and really enjoy all that is around you at the present moment. Have you ever just stopped and watched an animal going about its daily routine? If not, ask yourself why not. We can get so much pleasure from nature, if only we would let ourselves.

So let us look now at why it is good to get outdoors more often. Here are a few of the reasons I like to get outside.

You will find that your focus increases. The fresh air helps you to step away from everything and to refocus naturally on your tasks. Spending a few minutes outdoors every day can help you to regain your focus and will enable you to concentrate more on your work. You will also have better mental clarity and a longer attention span.

If you are looking for an instant stress release go outside and breathe in some fresh air. See how much better you feel after this. Taking short breaks from the things that are causing you stress will give you the boost that you need.

The outdoors has unseen therapeutic effects that actually increase your energy levels. It will also inspire you to move more. You can stretch your legs, which creates a greater development of coordination. You will be more active and this will encourage weight loss and help to maintain a stable weight.

Sunshine is packed full of vitamin D. Vitamin D is very important for maintaining a healthy immune system. It has been proven to help prevent osteoporosis, cancer and Alzheimer's. It may also help in the prevention of diabetes, multiple sclerosis, rheumatoid arthritis and heart disease. Supplements are not a substitute for the real thing. Go for the natural source in the sun. My tortoise laps up the sun. Why wouldn't you? Make sure you cover up or wear a sunscreen to protect your skin from the harmful rays.

Getting outdoors will give you an opportunity to forget about the phone, TV, internet and all the jobs that you need to do. It will enable you to get away, even if it is just for a few minutes.

How much time do you spend looking at a screen or at paperwork? This isn't so good for your eyes. When you get outside your pupils contract, similar to muscles, when looking at various distances. Your eyes have more scope than just looking straight in front of you. Walking around outdoors will give your eyes a chance to focus on the ground in front of you and at the landscape all around you. This is really good for over-stimulated eyes caused by screens.

## How to Enjoy Nature

You don't need to live in the country to feel the benefits. Wherever you are, step outside. It doesn't matter if you have 2 minutes or 2 weeks. Any amount of time outside is good for you.

Get outside in the fresh air. If you can get away from the smog and polluted air, do so. If this means having time away somewhere, try to do this as often as you can.

Take a few deep breaths. Breathe in the fresh air and feel it nourishing your body from your head to your toes.

Go for a walk or for a run or a cycle or WHATEVER. As long as you are outside it doesn't matter what the activity is.

Find a quiet place to sit and just be. Look at all the things around you. Notice the scenery and detail all around you. You may start to see things in your local area that you haven't noticed before and notice little animals and details you didn't know were there.

Close your eyes for a moment and picture what is around you. Hear the sounds as you picture it.

Live in the moment. Notice any sensations you feel on your body. It may be the feel of the wind or the rain or the sun. It may just be that you feel less tense in your muscles. Notice how your body feels in this time. Do you feel light or do you feel heavy? Do you have a spring in your step? Notice how you feel emotionally. Do you feel anxious or are you feeling relaxed and at ease? Noticing how you feel will give you insight into your current situation. Taking the time out may give you clarity of a situation and help you to think more creatively too.

Do something peaceful, such as meditating, fishing, yoga or even reading. You will start to notice all the natural sounds all around you as you relax and unwind.

Go camping.

Take a walk in the woods, up a hill, in a forest, by the sea or along a river or canal.

Look up at the stars and the moon.

Take your shoes and socks off and feel the earth, mud, grass or water between your toes.

Go for a picnic.

Think of all the things you did outside as a child. Could you do any of this now? Climb trees, swim in the sea, make daisy chains, fly a kite, run along the beach or how about playing frisbee or swingball. Have fun whilst you are outside and really let yourself enjoy the time.

By being out in nature you will find that you are not only relaxing and enjoying the surroundings but you will also deepen your connection to spirit. Take the time to get outside and enjoy it as often as you can.

# Chapter 37: Acts of Kindness

It is good for our spirit to give and to help others in some way. This doesn't have to be through the giving of money. It could be the kindness of your words. It could be the giving of your time, energy or ideas to help someone out. When did you last do something to help someone out in some way? How did it make you feel and how did they respond?

Only yesterday I went shopping with my partner. We paid for parking yet didn't use it all. I could see a young man about to put his money into the machine to get a ticket. I yelled at the top of my voice and ran towards him waving the little ticket frantically at him. I can only imagine what he thought! I gave him the ticket so he could enjoy the time left on it. He was very surprised to get this offer and couldn't thank me enough. I walked away feeling very happy that I had made him smile, saved him some money and boosted his mood.

Helping others releases endorphins in your brain and will boost happiness – both yours and the person you are helping. I certainly boosted my mood for the rest of the day and I can imagine he was happy too. Since you will be experiencing more happiness, you will also be healthier.

Acts of kindness help to build stronger communities. They aid with trust and co-operation between people and build a sense of safety in the community. They build an environment where people look out for each other and are more loving in their interactions. They are also a way to connect with others and provide a source of support (both for the person you are helping, the community and for you).

You will have heard the saying 'what goes around, comes around'. By giving you are opening yourself up to receiving.

**Acts of Kindness**

These must show genuine care and thoughtfulness. They should not be based around thinking about what you will get in return.

Here are a few thoughts to get you going on what you can do to help others. Remember it doesn't need to cost anything monetary wise!

Smile

Encouragement of some form

Kind words and sincere compliments

Say thank you

Give up your seat on public transport

Pick something up that someone has dropped

Help carry something – shopping, for instance

Give your parking ticket to someone else if it has time left on it

Share your newspaper or magazine with others

Let a car go in front of you in a queue

Hold a door open

Make someone laugh

Give a hug

Listen to someone attentively when they are talking – whether they are a stranger or not

Make someone new feel welcome and at ease

Help someone who is lost or wants directions

Have a conversation with a stranger

Let someone have your parking space

Treat a loved one to breakfast in bed

Invite a neighbour round for a drink and a chat

Pass on a book you have enjoyed

Bake something for a neighbour or relative

Let the people around you know how much you appreciate them

Visit someone who is feeling ill or lonely

Forgive someone for past events

Get in touch with someone you haven't spoken to for a while

## Over to You

Why not have a day where you focus on being kind to others? You will notice when you start, you will struggle to just do it on the one day. You will want to do it every day and as a result you will feel happier and healthier.

There are so many ways to give and to do things for others. Kindness doesn't cost a penny. It takes a thought and following through on that thought.

What could you do today to make someone smile?

## Chapter 38: Create and Play

I often hear people say 'I don't have a creative bone in my body.' I believe that everyone is born to be creative in some form or another.

How we are creative differs from person to person. There are many different ways to be creative. Most people think of drawing when they think of being creative. Creativity doesn't have to involve being artistic. It could involve cooking, baking, the choice of the clothes you wear, the make up or accessories you wear or the way you style your hair. You could sew, knit, build something or grow something. You may even write, or construct poetry. It could be that you are creative involving music, photography or drama. Whatever the activity, we are all creative in some way, whether we acknowledge it or not.

Creativity isn't something that is taught. It is an instinctive act. Some days it may be with us. Other days we just might not feel creative. It waxes and wanes, just like the moon.

The important thing about being creative is to connect with your spirit. We are not being creative to make money or to show to others the product of our time spent. The aim here is to do it for you and not for others. Bear in mind also that you are not doing it for people to criticise or to judge. Your main reason is to reconnect with your spirit and to relax your body and mind.

### Why Get Creative?

Your creativity is important to who you are. It is a way to express yourself and to really explore your inner world. Being creative in one aspect of your life leads into you being more creative in all aspects of your life. I find I am able to be more creative in how I problem solve, how I approach my days and how I organise my holiday time. This all started from being a bit more creative when cooking, playing my guitar and choosing to dress the way I want (not the way others think I should dress). The more creative you allow yourself to be, the more you will feel at peace within you. You will notice that you feel more alive, refreshed, relaxed and more joyful day to day. Giving yourself just a few minutes every day to create and explore your talents will have an effect on all aspects of your life.

## How to Be Creative
Build time into your day to be creative. If it helps, stick to the same time every day. If it doesn't help, be creative whenever you want!

Get your environment right. Create a space where you can feel inspired and at ease. Make sure it is comfortable, clean and you have everything you will need to hand. This will eliminate the time and distractions you will face of trying to find something.

Don't try to be perfect in what you are doing. This will only stifle your creativity.

Learn new skills. Don't limit yourself to doing things that are in your comfort zone. Step outside your comfort zone whenever possible. This is where real growth occurs and you will start to see changes in your life.

Do something you really enjoy and that you are good at. Forget the things that you think you should do or the things you don't enjoy. You will just wish away the time you spend doing it. Find something that you can really get stuck into and lose yourself in.

Do something you have always wanted to do. It may be trying your hand at pottery, learning how to play an instrument or cooking something different. Whatever it may be, don't put it off any longer. Live the life you want now.

Take time to develop yourself personally. Read a few books on personal development. Think about what areas of yourself you would like to work on and which areas you would like to grow in. Without growth, you will remain the same person for the rest of your life.

Read about new things. Choose to read something different such as spiritually uplifting books or creative books on subjects of your choice.

Stop watching television. It numbs your mind and fills it with negative images and thoughts.

Keep active. Take a walk outside. This might inspire you or at the very least, refresh your body and mind.

Get involved and make a contribution to something. How about a local play, musical or other live event? People organising and running events are always on the lookout for willing volunteers. Find something you would like to get involved in and volunteer.

Take out the crayons and a piece of paper. Draw whatever comes to mind. Stick it on the fridge to remind you of the fun you had.

Capture pictures or collect images that inspire you and post them on your walls.

Create a vision board. Fill it with all the things you want to be, do and have in your life. You may stick images you have collected, you may draw or you may add words or phrases to it. Look at it every day to remind you of what you want in your life.

Live in the moment. Really enjoy the experience and the time you have being creative. Avoid watching the clock. This will only make you feel stressed and stop you from living in the moment.

Being creative really nourishes the whole being. If you want to be happier, healthier and enjoy life to the full look at opportunities where you can become more creative in your life.

## Over to You

Think now about where you are already creative in your life. What do you do? What areas have you wanted to explore for a while but haven't quite got around to yet? Think about these areas and identify what you could do to become more creative in your days. It will be a worthwhile investment of your time and energies.

## Chapter 39: Balance Your Home and Work Life

### What is Balance?

Let us look at two different definitions of balance. One definition of balance is that it is 'an even distribution of weight enabling someone or something to remain upright and steady'. Another definition is to achieve 'a stable mental or psychological state; emotional stability'. Both definitions identify stability as the key theme.

When you think of balance do you think of weighing scales? If you add too much weight onto one side, the other side will go shooting up in the air. It knocks it off balance. This can happen to us as human beings too. We will look at balance in detail now and I will give you some ideas on how you can achieve balance at home, at work and to achieve balance between the two.

Our bodies strive for balance. Let me give you a practical example to demonstrate this. Physically, when it is cold we shiver to bring our body temperature up. When it is hot we sweat to bring our body temperature down. Our bodies are well adapted to fluctuations (be it temperature or anything else that might affect it) and respond appropriately when the conditions around us change. We are able to maintain balance (or equilibrium as it is also known) by adjusting our bodies to the external environment we find ourselves in. This is known as homeostasis.

We often hear that we need to achieve balance in our lives to be healthy and happy. By this we mean taking appropriate action to maintain equilibrium. In essence, this means that you have a handle on the various elements within your life. It means you don't feel that your heart or mind are being pulled too hard in any particular direction and you are at peace within yourself.

When you are balanced, more often than not, you feel calm, grounded, clear-headed and motivated to achieve your goals. It is important to realise that one person's idea of balance may not be the same as another's. It is a very individual thing.

Balance can be divided into two distinct areas, the internal and the external. By internal I mean anything related to the mind, heart and your health. By external I mean anything relating to work, relationships and activities you participate in. People generally focus on one side more than the other, without realising.

Have a think now. Do you achieve balance between the following?

### Internal Aspects
**Mind:** do you find a balance between challenging yourself intellectually and creating opportunities for your mind to rest?
**Heart:** do you balance giving love with receiving love?
**Health:** do you balance eating, drinking and exercising properly with resting and treating yourself to tasty things?

### External Aspects
**Work:** do you find a balance between pushing yourself to achieve your goals and seeing the bigger picture and enjoying the journey?
**Social:** do you balance being social with taking time out for yourself?
**Family:** do you balance fulfilling your family responsibilities with creating healthy boundaries?
**Fun:** do you balance allocating time for things you enjoy doing with making sure you don't overdo it?

Both sides are positive but if either side is taken to one extreme or the other, something that is intended to be positive can end up being detrimental to both your health and your relationships.

## Why Do We Need Balance?

Your body strives for balance to live a healthy life. All areas of your life are important and none of them should be neglected in any way. Your body, mind and spirit are all connected. You need to make sure all these three aspects are balanced. Different areas in your life are intertwined and neglecting one area can harm other areas in your life. If you are not paying attention to certain areas in your life, you will feel out of control.

Practicing the art of balance can bring more happiness into your life. It is not about reaching an end point of balance. It is about experiencing it along the whole life journey.

## Consequences of Imbalance

**Your health will be affected.** It may not affect you right now but it will inevitably catch up with you at some point in the future. Think of the people you know who have worked excessively hard and eaten really badly all of their lives for it to catch up with them later on in life. They have battered and bruised their bodies so much that it just can't take anymore and lets them know through illness or disease. We all know people who have done this and have faced illness (sometimes very serious illness) as a result.

Don't forget that you are the only one that can look after you. You need to take care of yourself. If you are leading an imbalanced life it can lead to stress, physical illness, depression and mental illness. It may not happen straight away but it will catch up with you eventually.

You will lose time with your family and friends. Communication and relationships can suffer as a result of imbalance in the different areas of your life.

You are most productive when you are relaxed. The harder you work, the less effective you will be. You are the most productive when you are not stressed. People often think they don't have time to take the time out. Yet when they do they are 100% more effective and focused. As well as feeling refreshed, motivated and happier in all aspects of their life.

If you regularly work long hours or work from home when the working day is finished, people will expect it from you more often. You could also be given more responsibility.

You may find that you are absent from work more often, you have increased errors when you are there or suffer from a lack of motivation and engagement.

Balancing your home, social and work life is essential for you to feel in control and to ensure you are happy and healthy all throughout your life.

## What Can Cause Imbalance?

There are many aspects that can cause imbalance in your life. These are the ones my clients have detailed to me over the years. Which ones can you identify with?

- Too many hours and energy spent at work.
- Not enough exercise, good food and time with family and friends.
- Focusing on the needs and priorities of their husband or wife and children instead of their own health.
- Poor communication with those around them.
- Saying yes to everything even if they know it's not possible.
- Inefficiency. Getting bogged down in all of the detail or being distracted by other things.
- Technology distracting them from the task at hand.
- Money. The need or desire to bring money in overrides everything in their life. .
- Unachievable deadlines.

- High workload and taking on other people's workload.
- Not being able to delegate jobs to others.
- Taking uncalculated risks.
- Not enough time alone – to relax, unwind, to reflect and put things into perspective.

Many other things can cause imbalance. These are just a few ideas to get you thinking.

## Over to You

Have a think now. What situations make you feel out of balance? Can you add any to the list above? And how are you when you are out of balance? What thoughts do you have? How do you act? How does your body respond as a result?

Make a note of these things to help raise your awareness of when you are out of balance. If you can spot the early signs that you are starting to be knocked off balance, you can make changes quickly to get you back on track.

## ♥ Achieving Balance at Home

Here are some ideas now on how you can achieve balance in your home life. In a nutshell, practice everything I have already talked about in the spirit section to this point! All of the points addressed so far will help you to feel more balanced at home (and at work!) A reminder of previous points covered and a few extras are below.

First and foremost, nurture yourself. Read the first chapter in the spirit section once again. All of these things are important to helping you to achieve balance in your home life.

Get out into the fresh air every day. Spend some time in nature.

Look for some time and space to get quiet and to think.

Think positively. Reframe any negative thoughts you are having.

Keep things in perspective.

Plan a weekend out of some sort every so often. Treat yourself!

Spend time with friends and family who make you feel good.

Do something that makes you feel good guilt free.

Find a hobby that you can enjoy.

Enjoy being in the moment. Enjoy what you are doing fully.

Manage your time. Organise all your household tasks efficiently, such as putting in a load of washing every day rather than saving it all for your day off. Put family events on a weekly family calendar to remind you what is coming up and keep a daily to-do list to keep on top of things that need doing. Do what needs to be done and let the rest go.

Take a day off. Remember a day off is a day off. Devote these entirely to things that make you feel good or important non-work responsibilities. Real days off rejuvenate, re-centre and recharge you, so that when you return to work, you are ready to rock again. Use them wisely.

Take a holiday. Allow yourself extended periods of time where you leave work behind and immerse yourself thoroughly in life.

## Achieving Balance at Work

The cumulative effect of increased working hours alongside the belief that you have to work long hours to climb the career ladder is having a profound effect on the lifestyle of a huge number of people all across the world. This is also likely to prove damaging to their mental and physical wellbeing. The number of people taking stress related sick leave is rising in the UK and (at the year of publication) costs the British industry approximately £370 million every year, which is approximately 91 million working days. This is half of all days lost. Crazy eh?

Here are some thoughts for how to achieve balance whilst you are at work and how you can make use of your time wisely.

Look at your daily schedule. Take a good look at your daily diary and the actions that are needed to be completed to highlight any inefficiencies that can be addressed. Can you do things in bulk or in a different way to make better use of your time? If so, this will reduce the time and energy wasted whilst you are at work.

Track your time. Write out your daily schedule and the amount of time that you want to devote to each activity. Stick to it. Decide what is necessary and what satisfies you the most or leads you to achieve your goals. If it doesn't relate to your goals think about why you are doing it.

Establish your priorities: think about what is urgent and important, non-urgent and important, urgent and not important and non-urgent and not important. Get a piece of paper and split it into four quadrants. Write the titles noted above in each quadrant. Write down your tasks in turn in one of the four quadrants. Deal with the ones that are important and urgent first. We tend to spend most of our time in the non-urgent and not important section as a matter of default. Take a look at Stephen Covey's Time Management Matrix to get an idea of how this works and for more information.

Alternatively, you could think: what do you absolutely need to do, what is less important and what can be delegated. You will probably find that you are spending time on tasks that aren't essential or timely.

Rewrite your daily schedule to take into account these newly identified priorities. When you allow your daily diary to be driven by your priorities and not the other way around, you are likely to be more effective, less stressed and have more time on your hands to do the things that you want to do.

Be disciplined. The danger of meetings, telephone calls and emails is that if you aren't disciplined they can get off topic and waste your time. How many times have you been in a meeting that has been purely focused on the agenda without it going off on a tangent? I can honestly say I struggle to think of any! In your daily schedule, determine how much time to devote to these communications and stay on task and on time with them. Think of polite ways you can take the conversation back to the topic when it does go off piste.

Be focused. When you are working on a project or action be totally present in what you are doing. Don't be distracted by activities earlier in the day or what might happen later in the day. The more you can focus on the task at hand, the better job you will do, the more you will enjoy it and the sooner you will get it done.

Be productive. When you try to do many tasks at once they all suffer. Sorry to say it but it is true. Pick one task, set everything else aside, get the job done and then move on to the next task.

Control your use of technology. It is a common belief that technology, such as computers, mobile phones and email has made people more productive and efficient. In my experience, technology acts as a distraction that interferes with doing your job well. Research has also demonstrated that technology has added to the work/life imbalance of business people. Limit your use and check email at specific times of the day. Don't spend all day with your email open. It will distract you and waste a lot of your time.

Write a to-do list every night before leaving work and stick to it the following day. Cross things through when you have achieved them. There is something very satisfying about striking through on a to-do list!

Cut or delegate activities you don't enjoy or can't handle.

Don't be afraid to say no: you don't have to do everything. Learn to say no. This is a very important lesson that most people need to learn. Remember that it is alright to respectfully say no. When you stop accepting tasks out of guilt or a false sense of obligation, you will have more time for the activities that are meaningful to you and will lead you to your goals.

Organise yourself and your space so you know exactly where everything is. This will save time searching for that piece of paper that you have lost.

Make it clear when you can't be interrupted. If you have a task to do that you need to concentrate on for a period of time, adopt a system that shows people that they cannot interrupt you. There are a few ways you can do this. A visual way is a good one, such as using a flag. Place a flag on top of your monitor or somewhere prominent. Let people know that you cannot be distracted when this is on. Alternatively, if you use an online calendar that you share with colleagues, put on it that you are in a meeting. It is a meeting with yourself but an important meeting all the same.

Take proper breaks at work. Take at least half an hour for lunch (if you are allocated it) and get out of the workplace if you can.

Take personal responsibility for your work-life balance. This includes speaking up when work expectations and demands are too much. Employers need to be aware of where the pressures lie in order to address them.

Remember the 80-20 rule. It comes into play in every aspect of your life. Not everything has to be perfect. Know what needs to be and what can be 80% perfect.

Use your support system. At work, join forces with colleagues who can cover for you (and vice versa) when family conflicts arise. At home, enlist trusted friends and loved ones to step in with child care or household responsibilities when you need to work overtime or travel.

## ♥ Achieving Work/Life Balance

As long as you're working, juggling the demands of a career and your personal life will probably be an ongoing challenge. Consider these ideas to find the work-life balance that works for you:

Separate your work and your life, wherever possible. Live in the moment when you are away from work. Be fully present when you are at home. When you are experiencing life, allow yourself to be totally immersed in it, which means not allowing work to intrude (unless there's a crisis that requires your immediate attention).

Don't strive for perfection. Imbalance happens from time to time. You need to get to the point where you can recognise it. Don't beat yourself up. Just find a way to rectify it as soon as you notice it and get back on track.

Set yourself goals. One of mine for a while was to leave work on time at least two evenings a week. It soon became a habit.

Try to reduce work related stress, for example through exercise, relaxation or hobbies.

Recognise the importance of protective factors, including exercise, leisure activities and friendships. Try to ensure that these are not sacrificed for working longer hours. Ensure that you spend your spare time on these things.

Leave work at work. This is the one that most people struggle with these days. With the technology to connect to anyone at any time from virtually anywhere, there might be no boundary between work and home, unless you create it.
Don't check your work emails when you are not at work. If you respond, people will expect you to every time you are away from work.

267

Make a conscious decision to separate work time from personal time. When you are with your family, for instance, keep your laptop in your bag and put your work mobile away.

Set aside time at home when you aren't with your husband/wife or children and get the work done. Don't take a business call or respond to emails when you are, for example, at the park with your children or at dinner with friends. Separate your work from your personal life as much as you can.

Have technology discipline. Do you really need to be in constant contact with the office 24/7? Turn off your mobile or screen calls when you are at home or leave it at home when you are out enjoying life.

Try to ensure that a line is drawn between work and home. If you do need to bring work home, try to ensure that you only work in a certain area of your home and can close the door on it when you are finished.

Don't forget to look at what you have achieved at the end of every day and reward yourself in some way, however small this may be.

Take advantage of your options. Ask your employer about flexing your hours, a compressed work week, job sharing, telecommuting or any other scheduling flexibility. The more control you have over your hours, the less stressed you are likely to be.

Seriously consider a career change or working part-time if you find your job dominates your life and is affecting your health. You have the power to make the choice. Is your health more important or your salary?

## Over to You

It is time to reflect. Ask yourself the following questions and answer as honestly as you can.

- How much time do you spend at work?
- How much time do you spend at home?
- What do you do whilst you are at home?
- How much time do you spend thinking about work or doing work whilst you are at home?
- How much time do you want to dedicate to work whilst at home?
- How much time do you want to generate for life balance?
- How will you use your home time?
- What will you do to ensure you enjoy it and have fun?

Hopefully, when you have the answer to these questions you can start to readdress the balance, if necessary.

Achieving balance within all aspects of your life is fundamental to you living a happy and healthy life. Think about what you do now and what you could do to achieve balance. Is there one particular area that suffers more than others? If so, what could you do to improve the situation?

Only when you are aware of what you do now can you start to change things. What are you going to change?

## Quiz - How Well Do You Look After Yourself?

How many of these statements do you agree with? Be honest and go with your gut instinct.

I take care of myself every day. I give myself time out to relax, to nurture myself, to exercise and to meditate.

I watch less than one hour of television a day and focus on things that nourish my body, mind and spirit instead.

I can recognise when Caveman Dave is taking hold and I know a range of strategies that can help to minimise the stress and tension I feel.

I exercise at least 4 times a week for over 30 minutes.

I get enough sleep all week so when I wake I feel refreshed, energised and raring to go.

I love my body and am happy with my self-image.

I feel at peace and live in spirit 80% of the time. My ego is firmly behind closed doors, most of the time.

I am creative at least 4 times a week and I really enjoy the time when I am being creative.

I live in the present moment for 80% of the week.

I think mainly think positive thoughts and when negative thoughts enter my mind, I reframe them into positive thoughts.

I have fun and laugh all throughout the week.

I value myself and know where I am headed in my life.

I have a journal and use this to note down my feelings and emotions on different aspects of my life.

I am thankful for things every day and let people know that I appreciate them.

I use affirmations daily to focus my mind on positive motivating thoughts.

I visualise my life as I want it to be at least three times a week. I am starting to see my ideal life play out in front of my eyes.

I do things for others regularly and as a result I have great relationships with those around me.

I attract good things into my life and see opportunities opening up before me.

I get outside into nature at least three times a week and really enjoy being outside.

I am happy with the balance between my work and my home life. I feel in balance and in control of my life.

**Now, total up how many of these statements you agree with and read the corresponding description below.**

### 15 - 20

You make it a priority to look after yourself and this shows in your physical, mental and spiritual health. To take it to the next level look at ways that you can build on this. It may involve looking at how to simplify your life or getting rid of as many things that stress you as you can. Talk to people about what you are doing so they can reap the benefits too. Keep up the good work!

## 11 - 15

You are not doing a bad job of looking after yourself. There is some commitment there but this could definitely be improved. Take a look back at your answers to find out where you can make some improvements. Take one step at a time, choose one area to work on and build it into your life before you move on to the next one. You believe in looking after yourself but maybe you use time as an excuse? Whatever the excuse is, deal with it and start to implement things to improve the situation.

## 0 - 10

You are not really into looking after yourself, for whatever reason. You may feel unimportant or put others before yourself. It is time to start taking action and to take back the control in your life. Identify one thing you want to work on and put an action plan into place to do it. Don't make excuses or find reasons why you shouldn't do it. Just do it. You will start to see the benefits very quickly and all the time spent doing these things is very much well spent. Maybe start off by reading the 'value yourself' chapter one more time. This will give you some questions to think about and ideas on how to get started. Don't put it off, do it now.

## Summary

A range of different ideas and strategies have been presented for you to think about and to implement into your life so you can start to live in spirit more frequently. Which ones stood out for you and really resonated with you? Start to implement these ones now.

There were many questions posed in the section. Highlight these questions and grab yourself a notebook. Go back and revisit the questions, trying to answer them as honestly and as fully as you can. They are posed to help you to think about the past, present and future and for you to think about how you can change your life for the better.

Think about the strategies that were noted in the section and take the time to revisit these too. How can you implement the strategies with no fuss and as part of a sustainable lifestyle?

Work your way through all the questions and thoughts. Doing so will help you to be more self-aware as well as ensuring that you live in spirit more frequently.

Remember, you choose how you feel, act and behave. The first step is to raise your self-awareness. Once you know where you are now, you can then make positive changes going forwards.

Achieving balance is a sought after principle and a very tricky thing to do but one that, when mastered, will have a positive impact on your health, life and relationships. Only when you achieve balance can you be living in spirit and be the best that you can be. Make it a priority to work through the ideas presented, to answer the questions posed and to start implementing these into your life.

## Summary of Tools and Tips

Here is a reminder of all the tools, tips and exercises discussed in this section to help you to live in spirit more frequently.

- Nurture yourself. Do you prioritise looking after yourself?
- Use the law of attraction: what is it you want to attract in your life?
- Adopt a positive mental attitude: keep both a negative thoughts diary and positive lists to hand.
- Use affirmations daily.
- Live in the moment.
- Give yourself self-time: how do you spend your days? Look back at the 'realigning your activities' and 'what I like' list.
- Leave your ego at the door: what does your ego and spirit look like?
- Have fun everyday: what makes you happy and have fun? Live like children.
- Lift your mood. Choose only good ones.
- Value yourself: 'what are you good at' questions.
- Build relaxation into every day. What makes you feel relaxed?
- Meditate: simple and spirit.
- Visualise your future. Decide what you want and create it in your mind. Live it out like it is a reality.
- Practice gratitude: keep a gratitude diary and practice giving thanks daily.
- Journal: free writing activity.
- Get out into nature: helping to bring you back to spirit.
- Do something for others: daily acts of kindness.
- Create something: how do you express yourself?
- Achieve balance – in life, work and between the two.

# Last Words

Hopefully, you will have read the contents of this book with an open mind and really embraced some (if not all) of the ideas within it.

My aim was to introduce you to ideas on how to become healthier and happier so you can see the benefits in all aspects of your life.

By looking at diet, exercise, stress, living in spirit and achieving balance, I hope you have a more rounded approach and knowledge to what you can do to become healthier and happier.

I believe that to really feel on top of your game, you must approach it from a holistic angle. Looking at just one or two of these aspects in isolation will not make you the best person you can be. However, looking at all of the aspects, will.

If you have read this quite quickly and thought 'I will come back to this when I am ready or in the right place mentally' then make sure you do.

Your health is very important and if you neglect yourself or think 'it can wait', I can guarantee that you will regret it later down the line. It is only when you experience the negative effects of your physical or mental health that you will realise what you had. Don't take your health for granted. Take control and start to do things that will nourish your body, mind and spirit on a daily basis.

The tips and strategies that you have been introduced to here may not be new to you. If this is the case, let them act as a reminder and become part of your toolkit that you can call upon when you need them.

For those that this is new to, consider taking one tip at a time and integrate it into your life. Start off slowly and make sure each is integrated before introducing the next. Bit by bit you can start to improve your health, your happiness and start to feel on top of your game.

The ideas here can be implemented straight away and whilst some will give immediate benefits, others may give longer-term benefits that you don't notice until later on in time. If you don't see immediate benefits, however small, do not give up on it. Keep going. You will see the benefits maybe a few weeks or months down the line.

Try out the strategies and see which ones work for you. Some may not and that is fine. But at least give them a go before you dismiss them.

Remember that getting your diet right is where it all starts. Once you have mastered this, you will start to see the difference in both your physical and mental health. Make sure you prioritise eating well and keeping active every day. Be aware of what turns you into Caveman Dave and look at ways to minimise the stress you feel. Do things that nourish your spirit and really make it soar every day. Live in spirit and remember to look after yourself. After all, no one else will.

You are the one responsible for your health and wellbeing.

You have taken the time to read this, so now take the time to implement these things.

Enjoy the journey, live in the present moment as often as you can and watch yourself become the best you can be.

# About the Author

As an author, international speaker and advisor on nutrition, health and living a balanced lifestyle, Gina's profile has never been higher.

Her success at helping others comes from offering a holistic approach, comprising of advice on food, keeping active, reducing stress, achieving balance and looking after the spirit.

As well as finding success through speaking on an international stage and writing on nutrition and wellbeing, Gina runs health retreats, workshops, a Health Academy and Cooking School.

Today, Gina has established herself as a force to be reckoned with in the sphere of food, health and wellbeing.

From her base in the heart of West Yorkshire, Gina helps people all over the globe to achieve a healthy mind, body and spirit through simple, down-to-earth advice.

Website:       www.healthbygina.com

Twitter:        @HealthByGina

Facebook:    HealthByGina

# A Gift From Gina

Congratulations on reaching the end of the invaluable lessons contained within this book.

By reading all the way to the end, you have taken the first step on your journey.

You now have, in your hands and mind, the basics for you to live a happier and healthier life.

**Now it's time to put it all into practice!**

This is your personal invitation to access Gina's FREE **'How to Get a Healthier Body in 5 Weeks'** programme.

During these sessions, you will receive coaching that will help you to identify where changes need to be made in your life and highlight the key areas you need to focus on.

The aim? To help YOU to live a happier and healthier life.

**Take action today.**

Go to www.healthbygina.com/go/5weekgift to grab your gift!

## Start Your Journey Here

Made in the USA
Charleston, SC
18 March 2014